Mountain Biking Moab
Pocket Guide

Help Us Keep This Guide Up to Date

Every effort has been made by the author and editors to make this guide as accurate and useful as possible. However, many things can change after a guide is published—trails are rerouted, regulations change, facilities come under new management, etc.

We would love to hear from you concerning your experiences with this guide and how you feel it could be improved and kept up to date. While we may not be able to respond to all comments and suggestions, we'll take them to heart and we'll also make certain to share them with the author. Please send your comments and suggestions to the following address:

The Globe Pequot Press
Reader Response/Editorial Department
P.O. Box 480
Guilford, CT 06437

Or you may e-mail us at:

editorial@GlobePequot.com

Thanks for your input, and happy trails!

Mountain Biking
Moab Pocket Guide

42 of the Area's Greatest
Off-Road Bicycle Rides

Second Edition

David Crowell

FALCONGUIDES ®

GUILFORD, CONNECTICUT
HELENA, MONTANA

AN IMPRINT OF THE GLOBE PEQUOT PRESS

FALCONGUIDES®

Falcon and FalconGuides are registered trade-
marks of Morris Book Publishing, LLC

A fat/trax® book.

ISSN 1545-9756
ISBN 978-0-7627-2799-5

Printed in the United States of America
Second Edition/Fifth Printing

To buy books in quantity for corporate use
or incentives, call **(800) 962–0973**
or e-mail **premiums@GlobePequot.com**.

Contents

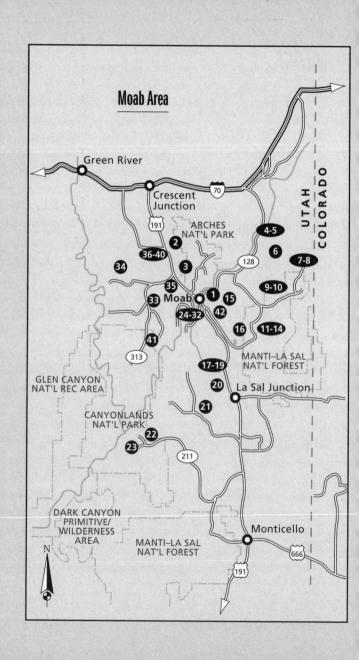

Moab Area

Green River

Crescent
Junction

70

191

ARCHES
NAT'L PARK

2

36-40

34

3

35

33 Moab

41

313

4-5

128

6

7-8

9-10

1

15

42

24-32

16

11-14

17-19

20 La Sal Junction

21

MANTI–LA SAL
NAT'L FOREST

GLEN CANYON
NAT'L REC AREA

CANYONLANDS
NAT'L PARK

22

23

211

DARK CANYON
PRIMITIVE/
WILDERNESS
AREA

MANTI–LA SAL
NAT'L FOREST

Monticello

666

191

UTAH
COLORADO

N

Acknowledgments

Where to begin? This would not have been possible without my editor, Will Harmon. Thanks for having faith in me!

The town of Moab took me in and shared its energy. It's a special, spiritual place. Moab's bike shops and their personnel kept me up and running through more than 1,000 miles of desert pounding.

Jay Stocks, I was honored to be part of your family. Amanda and Stephen were an unexpected joy! I wish you, Amy, and family well.

I also thank:

- Larry, Ned, Jennifer, Donovan and Monika, Patrick, Anthony, Chip, Rhonda, Rene, Lisa, Harry, Chase, Heather, Timothy, Judy Pentz, Harris the Cozmic Hitchhiker, T'uellan, Mike, Christie McNeil, Dan, Joe Hendrickson, and everyone else who listened to me babble from my barstool.

- Eddie and Audrey Snyder and the White Rim crew: Lisa, Lisa, Dennis, Donna, Steve, Honga, Corinne, and Angela.

- The radio personalities Christie Williams, Keith Simpson, the vinyl dinosaur, Scotty-O, Tim, and Bon Kelly.

- Eddie McStiff's for taking me in, Mondo's for keeping me awake, and KZMU for letting me be a DJ.

- My brother, Clint, for the morale boost after 500 miles of desert heat and the unconditional support.

- My mom for letting me watch the house and "finish" the book, and my dad for calling me there and keeping me sane.
- Scott Adams, Dave Montgomery, Ron George, Chad Niehous, and Glen Casamassa for their help with this update.
- My wife, Heidi, and our son, Dawson, who at ten weeks old visited his first two national parks during this update!
- The Earth Mother for giving me a place to play, laugh, and love.

Get Ready to CRANK!

Welcome, pilgrims, to the promised land. The land of standing rock, the *Toom'pin wunear Tuweap*. For seasoned riders and neophytes alike, this is where all trails eventually lead. This is the landscape our bikes were made for.

If Moab is the mecca for mountain biking, the reason is slickrock. Here huge beds of ancient sandstone have been carved by wind and water into a maze of canyons, plateaus, pillars, and walls. Slickrock, however, is anything but slick. Tires cling to it like paint to canvas, encouraging amazing feats of fat-tire artistry. Riding here will improve your skills and open your mind to new knobby possibilities.

Sculpted by nature, the land surrounding Moab provides a plethora of places to pedal. Mesa tops, canyon floors and rims, and the passes between cover environments ranging from open desert to old-growth juniper forests. The riding surface is just as varied. A single ride may roll over slickrock, sand, ledgy bedrock, mud, and cobblestones.

While the Slickrock Trail may be the point to the pilgrimage, slickrock snacks are offered in many canyons. But slickrock candy is only one entree of the region's menu to feed your mountain-biking soul.

The Manti–La Sals offer singletrack as rugged as the riders who call Moab home. And stump-jumping isn't just a trademark here, it's a sought-after thrill. These old volcanos never erupted, but their trails stoke a primitive mountaineering fire. Rocky, remote, and steep, they offer a cool alternative to the desert playground below.

As you worship this holiest of mountain-biking lands, keep in mind that, as rugged as they may look, some surfaces were not created to bear the brunt of tires. *Cryptobiotic crust,* a living topsoil, can be destroyed by just one errant tire. And some of the hard-packed roads turn to gumbo when wet. With so many fat-tire enthusiasts coming to Moab, we must all tread lightly. Read the section on the desert environment and be an educated rider. Stay on the trail.

Your pilgrimage to Moab will be rewarded. Services are held daily here, and they're a blast!

Welcome to the promised land.

The Journey

The journey of 1,000 miles begins with the first turn of the cranks.

Many who make the pilgrimage to Moab do so with their own vehicles. From the south there is only one real route choice, U.S. Highway 191. From the north there are two choices: US 191 or Utah Highway 128.

From the west, travelers eastbound on Interstate 70 should take exit 180 at Crescent Junction, which is 8 miles past the roadside town of Green River. From the east, travelers westbound on the interstate have a more scenic option. The second Cisco exit, exit 202, is for Utah 128. This is known locally as The River Road because it parallels the Colorado River and skirts huge sandstone cliffs before joining US 191 just north of Moab. This road also features the Bureau of Land Management's Colorado Riverway campsites, Matrimony Spring, and a junction with the La Sal Loop Road.

From Denver, drive west on I–70 for six or seven hours to exit 202 or exit 180 and follow the above directions. If your gas gauge is lower than a quarter in Grand Junction, it's smart to fill up.

From Salt Lake City, drive south on Interstate 15 past Provo. Get off at exit 261 after passing Springerville and drive south on U.S. Highway 89, which leads to Thistle. Soon after, take U.S. Highway 6 south past Price and Wellington, where it becomes US 191. Follow US 191 into Green River and onto I–70. Go east to exit 202 and then drop south on US 191 into Moab.

If your journey to Moab begins by air, Canyonlands Airport has service from Denver and Phoenix that, at last check, allowed bikes to travel for free. The airport is 19 miles north of Moab on US 191.

Other air options include flying into Salt Lake City, Utah (236 road miles to Moab), or Grand Junction, Colorado (110 miles). Shuttle services are available from both these locations, as are rental vehicles.

Moab

Moab is a great town. It is full of people that are friendly and nonjudgmental. If they are treated with respect, they'll return the courtesy.

Many residents also feel their town has been turned upside down in the past few years from tourists. While this isn't the lone fault of bikers, we are far from blameless. It may seem innocent enough to go in and fill water bottles at a store, but the shopkeepers aren't in business to wet the innumerable whistles of visiting bikers for free. Always ask before filling bottles, and do so only if you buy something. Better still, the bike shops are more understanding and willing to help. Use them.

There are some public places to fill up. City Park on 100 West and 400 North has some water spigots, as does Lion's

Park on the corner of US 191 and Utah 128. About 0.1 mile down Utah 128 from Lion's Park is Matrimony Spring, a popular watering hole. Another popular spring is at mile 2.2 of Hurrah Pass (Ride 26).

Another water-oriented plague for Moab is dust-caked campers looking for showers (see Appendix C).

The good news is that many places cater to the every need of tourists. This includes food, coffee, rooms, showers, rental jeeps, laundromats—everything a big city could boast, at reasonable prices.

A couple of grocery stores are on Main, and a health-food store is near Rim Cyclery on 1st West (100 West). And there's always Dave's Corner Market at Mill Creek Drive and 400 East.

More good news is the radio station. No longer is the choice limited to Muzak and religious programming. A wide variety of real music is played on Moab's own FM station, KZMU 89.7. Call in a request (259–4897), and it's a good bet it'll be played.

The town now has its own skatepark located in the northeast side of City Park. It's open to bikes and boards.

Probably your first stop in town is the visitor center. Located at Main and Center Streets, this is an excellent place to get oriented. They have maps, books, museumlike displays, and an informative staff with links to all the land-management agencies. Campground availability and the weather forecast are posted here. A message board between the visitor center and Eddie McStiff's is a good way keep your group a group.

Hopefully you won't need to know that Moab's hospital is located at 719 West 400 North. The phone number is 911 or (435) 259–7191.

Party Time!

If you come to Moab to party, think first about Utah's liquor laws. First of all . . . don't drink and drive (or pedal). Beyond that, Utah has some rules pertaining to demon alcohol that will have many folks baffled. How do you find a drink in Moab?

Well, these rules change as often as a newborn's diapers. At press time it worked like this: Hard alcohol (such as whiskey), wine, and normal beer are available at the state-run liquor store next to Arby's restaurant, a block west of Main Street. Plan ahead—the beer is expensive and sold warm.

Beer is also sold in convenience stores, grocery stores, and to-go from microbreweries such as Eddie McStiff's. All of this is 3.2 percent alcohol, which means it's a bit weaker than the standard brew.

There are three places to be served drinks: taverns, clubs, and some restaurants. A tavern can sell 3.2 percent beer; that's it. A club can sell the hard stuff to members and their guests. A restaurant with the proper license can sell the hard stuff provided the patron is actually eating. Your server can't show you a wine list unless you ask for it.

But wait, it's not that simple. An establishment may contain a tavern and a restaurant and may sell only beer at the bar (tavern) and hard stuff to those who eat in the restaurant. Just ask where to sit to be served what you want. The advantage to the system is that Moab has some great microbrews available. Try the Cisco Stout. It's a complete meal in itself.

A club can serve only members and their guests. If you're not a member, you must be sponsored by a member. This is accomplished by going into the club and trying to get served. They will take care of the rest. It feels awkward at first, but the spirits will flow. Of course, flow is a relative term. Liquor can be doled out only one ounce at a time. No doubles and only one drink at a time.

Think these rules are strange? Try ordering meat that is medium-rare. Go ahead, try it. Honest.

Bike-Shop Heaven

Moab probably has more bike shops per capita than any-where else on the planet, so it well equipped to handle all a biker needs. While its official population is just shy of 5,000, Moab offers more biking amenities than most big cities. Five bike shops carry everything from patches to full-suspension, high-dollar rigs. What this means in the real world is good service and competitive prices. It also means lots of good advice on equipment, rental rigs, trail updates, tours, and shuttle information. Each shop has its own feel, and some even have espresso!

Shelter

Moab has a hotel/motel guest capacity of at least 1,800. That seems like a lot for a town this size. Heck, it certainly looks like enough during a tour down Main Street. But during the season it is very hard to find a room.

Rooms run the gamut of budget to luxurious. Many of the high-end rooms are found in bed-and-breakfasts. Ask about bike-related rules. Most proprietors in this mountain-biking mecca are enlightened, but some establishments still have a few archaic practices. "Can I store my bike in my room?" is a good question to ask. Currently, crime isn't a big problem in Moab, and practicing normal bike security is usually enough. But you never know. Spring and fall are certainly the riskiest times.

Recreational vehicle campgrounds offer sites in and out of town. They have showers and tent camping available. Bureau of Land Management (BLM) and La Sal National Forest lands offer a couple of pay camping sites as well. (See Appendix E.) The visitor center at Center and Main in Moab posts the current status of national park and forest service campgrounds.

Showers

There comes a time when all riders must remove the deposits of trail and perspiration accumulated upon their persons. This act has been a major cause of friction between Moabites and bikers. Unfortunately, the mountain biker's pioneering spirit, which causes us to seek novel ways to overcome diversity, can hinder public relations when applied to showering.

Yes, it is possible to clean one's self in the sink of a public establishment. But it ain't too cool. Think about it. The sinks in Moab are not there so bikers can prove how innovative they are at saving money. Think about the karma of the situation . . . before it breaks your chain in the middle of the desert.

Appendix C lists places that encourage showering for a fee. This can run from $2.00 to $5.00, which still makes for a cheap stay.

Being Prepared

Mountain Biking Moab Pocket Guide is a where-to-ride book. How to ride is another story. What to bring lies in the gray area between the two subjects. Common sense is the rule here. Bring what makes you feel comfortable. If you need a personal mechanic to follow you, pay Cycle Sean to do so.

If you like to ride in just shorts and a hat, well, it's your body. But here are a few ideas on equipment, tools, first aid, clothing, water, and weather.

Equipment

Technoweenies live for places like this! Any piece of gear that was dreamed up for mountain biking probably had Moab in mind. A necessity is a small chainring or a climbing gear. You can climb incredibly steep angles of slickrock if you've got a gear low enough for your legs to spin. If the biggest rear cog (gear) is 28 or smaller, then the small chainring on the front should be 22 or smaller.

It's also important to have a way to carry lots of water. Two cages with large water bottles is the minimum. A backborne hydration setup is ideal.

Other equipment, like shocks, makes things nicer, but the gear ratio is most important.

The local bike shops have a range of rentals available to those who arrive sans bike or have discovered their own equipment is lacking.

Tools

Tools are a touchy subject for bikers—each has his or her own opinion. The riding here is torturous on equipment. Rock can peel the knobbies right off a tire and eat the derailleur for dessert. Keep one question in mind: "What's the farthest I'd have to walk?" I weigh out the tools and my desire not to walk, which usually results in this list.

Sense of humor—perhaps the most important item

Spare tube—for the first flat

Patch kit—for additional flats

Air pump—to reinflate ego after a particularly technical section

Allen wrench—to fend off rabid rodents
Channel locks—a moment of silence for the ultimate tool
Spare cables—a fancy, long one with both brake and derailleur ends
Chain tool—I secured a crank with one of these!
Pocket knife—to protect that last energy bar from scavengers
Duct Tape—wrap a supply around the seat post...and bow down before it.
Headlamp or flashlight—to walk home after dark

If you can't replace a tube without tire levers, bring them too. You can always just bring $5.00 and hope it buys a repair. This list is minuscule for some and totally foreign to others. I've seen wonders done with nothing more than energy bar wrappers. Just remember that, with time, everywhere is within walking distance.

First Aid

Consider packing a first-aid kit. The most important item to put in the kit weighs nothing: prevention. Remember that safety is your responsibility. Read up on desert hazards and know your biking limits. Then ask yourself, "How far will I be from help?" and pack accordingly. Around Moab, help is hindered by the very terrain that brings us here. You could notify someone of your problem and still be stuck overnight. Here is a partial list to consider:

Butterfly-closure bandages
Adhesive bandages
Gauze compress pads and gauze wrap
Allergy pills
Emergency water purification tablets

Moleskin
Antiseptic swabs
Sunscreen
Energy bar
Emergency blanket

The best thing to bring is a riding partner. Riding alone in remote areas isn't wise. If you do have a bad crash or succumb to the heat, cold, lightning, wild animals, or act of God, remain calm and make decisions with a clear mind. Also remember the primary rule of first aid: do no harm. This means doing only what you must to keep the injured person alive and as comfortable as possible until you can get to a doctor. With luck you may run into help on the way out (and a pox on those who don't offer help). The point is don't waste time and don't panic. Deal with things as they come up and keep going.

Always wear a helmet. Slickrock facials are no fun. But they are worse with a naked melon. Those buff quads and powerful lungs won't go far without a brain to guide them. Some other cycling apparel also makes sense from a first-aid standpoint. Gloves will save your hands from scrapes and cuts, and cycling shorts save your butt.

Sun

The desert sun does more than just create a need for water. It can literally cook you!

Sunburn is easy to combat. Use a sunscreen of at least SPF 15 thirty minutes before going out and reapply it frequently. Pay particular attention to your nose, cheekbones, ears, and the nape of your neck. Sun-sensitive riders will want to take more extreme measures to blot out the sun.

Some experts suggest long-sleeved, loose-fitting, white clothing. Be sure your clothing doesn't lead to a second hazard, overheating.

Heat exhaustion is a prominent danger, especially in summer when temperatures above 100 degrees Fahrenheit are common. Just being hydrated is not enough. Sometimes the body just can't keep up with rising temperatures, and its cooling system shuts down. Warning signs include pale skin, heavy sweating, nausea, weakness and dizziness, thirst, headache, and muscle cramps. If you experience any of these symptoms, find shade immediately and cool off as well as possible. Douse your head and chest with water (save some for drinking) and try to keep air moving over your skin. If you try to ride through heat exhaustion, you'll likely end up with heat stroke, a far more serious—and often fatal—condition.

Always wear sunglasses to protect your eyes from sun, eye strain, kamikaze insects, and flying rocks spun up by your tires. A helmet visor also helps and will keep your eyes on the trail and the sun off your nose.

Of course the best ammo is prevention. During summer in the canyon regions (see summer options), plan to complete your ride by 9:00 A.M. The desert is intense. Show your respect.

Water

A human's weight is at least 80 percent water. A desert is defined by a significant lack of water. This makes for a simple rule. **Bring as much water as you can carry.** Also drink lots of water before riding. Many people drink far too little water before heading out and are already dehydrated.

After you become an experienced desert rider, tailor how much fluid you bring on a ride. For now, however, bring all that can be carried. That means both water bottle cages full with large bottles, in addition to a back-borne water bladder.

Odds are someone in your group will run out or start rationing. Share rather than ration. It's also a good idea to bring something to replenish electrolytes, too. Use the back-borne bladder for water and the bottles for electrolyte drinks. And keep an extra gallon or two in the car for après-ride rehydration

Of course, carrying lots of water does nothing if it's just along for the ride. A body in the desert is said to need more than a gallon of water a day. Add a bit of strenuous exercise and do the math. Drink lots and drink often. Lungs dump huge amounts of moisture into exhaling breath, which, combined with sweating, quickly dehydrates the body. Don't run a quart low. Drink!

For information on water found on the trail see the "Riding Right" section later in this chapter.

Weather

Moab's weather can be as extreme as its landscape. But the biggest concern for bikers, besides the baking sun and broiling heat, are the sudden storms that sweep across the desert. Intense thunder-boomers bring deadly lightning, strong winds, and wash-filling rains. When thunderheads start forming, head to town and enjoy the local ambience.

If caught in a storm, some precautions can help keep you safe. Check how close the lightning is with the old trick of counting the seconds between the flash and the thunderclap. A count up to "five-Mississippi" means the last flash was about 1 mile distant. If you hear thunder it's possible to be struck, and it's time to take cover. When in the open, ditch your bike and other metal objects. Then find a place to hunker down. Don't be the tallest thing around, and do not hide under the lone tree. The idea is to reduce your contact with the ground and avoid being a lightning rod or hiding under one. Look for a depression or low point and crouch (don't lie down). Try to avoid puddles and moving water. It's easy to feel exposed in Canyon Country, but don't panic.

If you duck into a dry wash or canyon to avoid lightning, be alert for flash floods. Flash floods in the desert are beautiful events. Instant rivers shoot off of slickrock cliffs, carving their paths just a bit deeper. But these same waters are downright ugly when you're in their path! The key is awareness. A flood can sweep through even when it's not raining in your area. Water can travel far in a desert down twisting washes. Listen to the radio for flash-flood warnings, and heed them. If caught in a flood, don't try to outrun it. Get out of the wash to higher ground and wait. Enjoy its beauty and don't tempt fate.

Rain can also turn local soils into a sticky glop that is a cross between Marshmallow Fluff and B-movie swamp slime. It's slicker than snot and gloms on to anything it touches. The soils northwest of town seem to be worse than elsewhere after a rain. Rides 3, 7, 32, 38, and 39 should be avoided during and immediately following rain. The rain does make the sand easier to ride! Right after a storm is great for Poison Spider and the extremely sandy rides. But beware, slickrock is temperamental when wet and can live up to its name.

Spring tends to bring a flurry of dramatic storms; summer storms are less frequent. Fall storms are less violent but usually colder.

When to Ride

The most common times to ride are spring and fall when throngs of riders pour in from across the globe.

Spring tends to run from college break until the "no-see-ums" (annoying, biting flies) show up in late May. The trails are most crowded during this season.

Fall starts with the falling temperatures of mid-September and lasts as long as the weather stays nice. The annual Fat Tire Festival in Moab coincides with Halloween, but the weather can be pretty cold by then.

Winter sees few riders, but the riding can be nice. Although snow can and does occur, many days bring calm air and a warm sun, making riding a treat. The upper mesas and mountains are snow covered, but the lowlands are usually rideable. Sandy trails firm up from frost, and the crowds are only a memory. Of course, patches of ice on slickrock and changing weather are factors to be reckoned with. In the past the town closed up shop in winter. Now you'll find a full range of services and off-season discounts.

Summer is also a time of fewer riders. The few who have ridden here in July know why! Temperatures above 100 degrees cook bikers as they search for shade. Any shade. To ride in the summer requires early starts (dawn's early light) and completing rides by 9:00 A.M. Some people ride in the evening, but so many factors make that dangerous that it's not recommended. If you do venture out after dark, however, a strong light with a full charge, an extra bulb, and an extra battery is a good idea . . . along with a full moon. If you're in Moab during summer, try riding in the La Sals. Temperatures there range in the low 80s and the terrain is awesome! Nights are cool, just right for camping.

Appendix D is a list of average temperatures to help you plan your riding season. Of course, as with all averages, anything can and does happen.

Riding Right!

The desert ecosystem is very fragile. Sure it seems rugged as it tears apart high-dollar bike rigs and their riders. But the land is fragile at heart. The ways humans can damage an environment are unlimited, but keeping it safe requires only respect and knowledge.

The basic building block of the desert is cryptobiotic soil. This is a fancy word for living dirt. It's chock-full of nutrients that feed the plants and even hold the dirt in place. It's like those twenty-three-chemical energy drinks racers are so fond of: You don't need to know how it works to benefit from it. At any rate, this crusty dirt is breakable. Just riding or stepping on it destroys the organisms within, leaving a scar for at least a decade and probably harming the area for fifty years. Luckily it's just as easily protected. Don't ride off trail, and if you walk off trail do so only on slickrock. Many people say they know what cryptobiotic soil looks like and can easily avoid it. The black, crusty castellations typical of one form are indeed easy to recognize, but these living soils also take many other forms that are virtually indiscernible from plain old dirt. If you walk off trail in the desert, you are most likely damaging cryptobiotic soil.

The next slice of tiny life involves water. You may actually find water on the trail occasionally, but do not use it. First of all, the potholes that catch rainwater are very important to wildlife. That includes the tiny waterborne creatures that hatch, mate, and die all in the short life span of the pothole. Bikers filling water bottles kill these creatures. Secondly, sweat, skin oils, and bike by-products (such as lube) all change the chemical makeup of the water. Wildlife can't go fill up at a faucet when they get back to town. You can. Don't use their water except in an emergency. Don't ride through or dip into the potholes.

The nature of springs and seeps allows a bit more interaction. They are often rock-filtered and quite fresh. However, unless you know that a particular spring is safe, don't drink from it. Matrimony Spring on Utah 128 is a popular watering hole, but it is unregulated. Another such spring is at mile 2.2 of the Hurrah Pass ride.

If you find yourself in a situation where you need to use the available water, be forewarned. This region has a wealth of minerals that dissolve in surface and groundwater. The human body does not cope well with some minerals, particularly when they're poured down the gullet in copious quantities. Arsenic, to name one, is not an elixir of life. It can cause cancer over the long haul and is toxic in higher doses over the short run. Most portable water filters do not remove arsenic, lead, and other toxic minerals. If you must drink the water, limit your intake to the amount needed to get you back to civilization. Use a filter to remove bacteria and other gut-loving life. Springs are the best bet, but stay away from anything near mine tailings.

Mountain-Biking Guidelines

If every mountain biker always yielded the right-of-way, stayed on the trail, avoided wet or muddy trails, rode in control, showed respect for other trail users, carried out every last scrap of what was carried in (candy wrappers and bike-part debris included) and never cut switchbacks—in short, if we all did the right things—we wouldn't need a list of rules governing our behavior.

The fact is most mountain bikers are conscientious and try to do the right thing; however, thousands of miles of dirt trails have been closed due to the irresponsible habits of a few riders.

Here are some basic guidelines adapted from the International Mountain Bicycling Association Rules of the Trail. These guidelines can help prevent damage to land, water, plants, and wildlife; maintain trail access; and avoid conflicts with other backcountry visitors and trail users.

1. **Only ride on trails that are open.** Don't trespass on private land, and be sure to obtain any necessary permits. If you're not sure if a trail is closed or if you need a permit, don't hesitate to ask.

2. **Keep your bicycle under control.** Watch the condition of the trail at all times, and follow the appropriate speed regulations and recommendations.

3. **Yield to others on the trail.** Make your approach well known in advance, either with a friendly greeting or a bell. When approaching a corner, junction, or blind spot, expect to encounter other trail users. When passing others, show your respect by slowing to a walking pace.

4. **Don't startle animals.** Animals may be easily scared by sudden approaches or loud noises. For your safety—and the safety of others in the area as well as the animals themselves—give all wildlife a wide berth. When encountering horses, defer to the horseback riders' directions.

5. **Have zero impact.** Be aware of the impact you're making on the trail beneath you. You should not ride under conditions where you will leave evidence of your passing, such as on certain soils after rain. If a ride features optional side hikes into wilderness areas, be a zero-impact hiker, too. Whether you're on bike or on foot, stick to existing trails, leave gates as you found them, and carry out everything you brought in.

6. **Be prepared.** Know the equipment you are using, the area where you'll be riding, and your cycling abilities and limitations. Avoid unnecessary breakdowns by keeping your equipment in good shape. When you head out, bring spare parts and supplies for weather changes. Be sure to wear appropriate safety gear, including a helmet, and learn how to be self-sufficient.

How to Use This Guide

Most of the information in this book is self-explanatory. But if anything in a ride description doesn't seem to make sense, re-read the following explanation of our format. There is also a glossary in the back.

The information is listed in an at-a-glance format. It is divided into twelve sections:

The **ride number** refers to where the ride falls in this guide. Use this number when cross-referencing between rides for an easy method of finding the descriptions. The ride name refers to the name of the trail. Where more than one name exists, one has been chosen that best reflects the nature of the trail.

Location tells, in general, where the ride is in relation to Moab.

Distance gives the ride's length in miles.

Approximate riding time is an estimate of how long it will take to complete the ride. It represents trail time and does not include stops. If the ride is rated more difficult or strenuous than what you usually ride, add some time to the estimate. If rated much higher, add a big chunk of time. The scenery and physical challenge of these rides warrant plenty of stopping. As you pedal through a few rides in this book, compare your ride times with those listed in the guide and adjust your estimates for future rides accordingly.

Physical difficulty estimates the physical challenge of the ride. The levels are easy, moderate, and strenuous. The following are descriptions of what went into the rating.

> **Easy:** Rides are mostly flat, but this may include some rolling hills. Any climbs will be short. *Easy rides around Moab are harder than what the locals may call easy in other places.*

> **Moderate:** Rides will have climbs; some may be steep. Strenuous sections may occur, but the majority of the ride is moderate. Even on a moderate ride, some steeper sections may force some cyclists to dismount and walk.

> **Strenuous:** Rides put the granny gear to work! The steeps may be long grueling tests of endurance, power, and determination.

Remember this region is tougher than most, and the ratings are for comparison between rides around Moab. Easy rides can still have you gulping air, and moderate ones may induce you to walk. Walking a bike is a perfectly legitimate way to transport it. Also remember that this guide is for everyone, from beginners to experts. Compare your first rides to the levels listed here to get a feel for the classifications. Also bear in mind that technical sections that exceed your ability will be tiring and can make an easy or moderate ride seem strenuous.

Technical difficulty is not a problem with your new antichain-suck device. It is a rating from easy to challenging that quantifies how much biking skill is needed to keep you in the saddle with the rubber side down. Specific reasons for the rating might be listed. *These ratings may seem low when compared to other regions; Moab's terrain may be tougher than anywhere on the globe.* What may be challenging in Alabama or Oregon could be moderate to challenging here.

Easy: Basic bike-riding skill needed for riding smooth and obstacle-free routes. No easy rides are in this guide. This is Moab!

Easy to moderate: Mostly smooth tread with minor difficulties. Ruts, loose gravel, or obstacles may exist, but they are easily avoided.

Moderate: Irregular tread with some rough sections, steeps, obstacles, gravel, sharp turns, slickrock, small ledge drops. These will have obvious route options or lines through them.

Moderate to challenging: Rough going! The tread is uneven with few smooth sections. The line is limited as it weaves through rocks (boulders, babyheads, basketballs), sand, eroded washes, downfall, slickrock snacks, bedrock ledges, and any combinations of them all. These obstacles often occur on steeps!

Challenging: Continuously broken, rocky, or trenched tread with frequent, sudden, and severe changes in gradient. Slopes necessitating off-the-seat riding and a nearly continuous barrage of obstacles where the line is tough to find and unforgiving if missed.

Again these ratings are for comparison's sake. Extreme obstacles may exist on any trail, and in this dynamic environment riders should be ready for obstacles at all times. Gauge your ability against the scale after your first few rides to get a feel for the ratings, and remember that different obstacles require different techniques.

Trail surface describes what the tires ride on when they are rubber-side down.

Highlights list where to find the ride's emotional story. Qualities that make the ride unique and any special notes will be listed here.

Land status lists the land-management agency. The rides in this guide are mostly on public lands. Appendix B gives the information needed to contact the various land-management agencies about rules, regulations, permits, and updates.

Maps include USGS maps that show each ride's area. These maps can be used for a more detailed view though they may not show the ride's route. Each Mountain Biking Moab map and profile should be more than sufficient for navigational and planning purposes.

Finding the trailhead tells you, well, how to find the trailhead. In most cases the directions begin from the Moab Visitor Center at the corner of Center Street and Main.

The ride lists where to go and how to find the way back. Attached to the descriptions are odometer readings. These are estimates! Not all bike computers are calibrated the same, but they provide a yardstick to measure against. In Canyon Country this can mean the difference between a fun ride and a dangerous night out in the desert.

The **elevation profiles** provide a good look at what's in store by graphically showing altitude change, tread, and ratings. The ups and downs of the route are graphed on a grid of elevation (in feet above sea level) and miles pedaled. Route surface conditions (see map legend) and technical levels are also shown on the graphs. The technical levels are rated as follows: 1, easy; 2, easy to moderate; 3, moderate; 4, moderate to challenging; 5, challenging. Pluses and minuses cover the inbetween areas. These are frequently used to distinguish between the many high-difficulty rides.

Note that these graphs are compressed (squeezed) to fit on the page. The actual slopes you will ride may not be as steep as the lines drawn on the graphs—it just feels that way. Also some extremely short dips and climbs are too small to show up on the graphs. All such abrupt changes in gradient are, however, mentioned in the mile-by-mile ride description.

The **maps** are clean, easy-to-use navigational tools. Closed trails are not usually shown but may be listed in the ride description. Painstaking effort has been taken to ensure accuracy. The nature of Canyon Country has led to these simplified maps. While each nook and cranny may not be depicted, sufficient terrain is shown to keep you on track.

This guide doesn't pretend to be omniscient. Ratings and ride accounts are as accurate as possible. However, everyone is different. Individual riders excel in different skills and have different tastes. Use the guide as a starting point. Though regulations, ownership, and even the land itself may change, this guide will help get you home in one piece. If you have an inadvertent adventure you want to share, drop me a line.

Map Legend

Trail		Interstate (70)	
Unimproved Road		U.S. Highway (191)	
Paved Road		State Highway (128)	
Gravel Road		Forest Road 207	
Interstate		Arch	
Wilderness Boundary		Bridge	
Waterway		Camping	
State Line		Gate	
Cliff		Mountain Peak/Elevation Point	
Lake/Reservoir		Parking	
Slickrock		Picnic Area	
Power Lines		Point of Interest	
Fence		Rest Room	
Railroad		Town	
		Trailhead	

1 The Slickrock Trail

Location: 3.6 miles east of Moab on Sand Flats Road.

Distance: 10.5-mile lariat-shaped loop with the practice loop (9.7 miles without). Numerous spurs and free-form exploring can increase mileage dramatically.

Approximate riding time: 1.5 to 5 hours. This isn't a misprint. Riders in excellent shape can crank this out in 1.5 hours. Others sometimes miscalculate the time it takes to walk the steeps. Don't be caught in the dark on the rock.

Physical difficulty: Strenuous. Most of the short pitches are amazingly steep. Your bike has the traction to climb them if you have the strength and technique to power it.

Technical difficulty: Challenging. The entire trail isn't one long trials maneuver. But any lapse of attention can mean a slickrock facial followed by a run to the emergency room. The technical spots are expert caliber with official danger sections marked with black diamonds in the painted dashes. Don't count on all the hazards being marked or described here!

Trail surface: 10.5 miles on slickrock. The geologically aware will get a laugh knowing that this rock is not of the actual Slick Rock formation. With the exception of an occasional sandy wash, the entire trail is on Navajo Sandstone marked with white dashes. Slickrock has come to mean any sandstone that holds bike tires like a pit bull holds a bone. In case you were wondering, the name slickrock comes from the fact that to shoed horses sandstone is slicker than snot on a glass doorknob.

Highlights: This is the ride that made Moab. The mix of strenuous wall climbs and hair-raising dips, half-pipes, and ledge drops on unbelievably high-traction sandstone will make you a changed rider. This is *The* Slickrock Trail. The promised land. The point to the pilgrimage. It is also crowded. Riding it during high season means waiting above the drops for a wave of riders to climb up, then descending with your own wave. It means playing leapfrog with other groups as each struggles to climb, drop, and maneuver around the loop. For those not held by a necessity to follow the lines, crowds can be avoided by exploring the un-dashed rock. Either way the views and thrills are unparalleled. If the trail frightens you, well, good. The hazards are fairly visible and therefore avoidable (walkable). This description chooses the "easier," clockwise, path gaining a big chunk of altitude on a steep pitch (aka "Cogs To Spare") that is usually walked anyway, making this direction seem less strenuous. Either way sees each and every obstacle. The numerous spurs and unmarked rock offer days of fun and are left undescribed to allow self discovery of the free-form playground that is slickrock. Sim-ply avoid crushing crust or poi-soning potholes. Enjoy!

Land status: BLM. The Commu-nity Sand Flats Team (435) 259-2444 is doing a determined job of maintaining order in the area while nature repairs itself from past abuses. If you want to camp up here, check out Appen-dix E.

Maps: USGS Moab; BLM Slick-rock Trail Map (free with access fee).

Finding the trailhead: From the visitor center parking lot at Center Street and Main in Moab, turn right onto Center. Go 0.3 mile east on Center and turn right onto 400 East. Go 0.4 mile south on this wide road to Mill Creek Drive and turn left (Dave's Corner Market is on the corner). Go another 0.5 mile to a stop sign, then continue straight through the intersection onto Sand Flats Road. A cemetery is on the left. This road passes "America's most scenic dump" to reach the Sand Flats Recreational Area gate in 1.8 miles. Pay the appropriate fee ($5.00 by car or $2.00 by bike [see Appendix F]) and continue 0.6 mile to the parking lot for the world's most famous bike trail. Total distance from downtown to the trailhead is 3.6 miles.

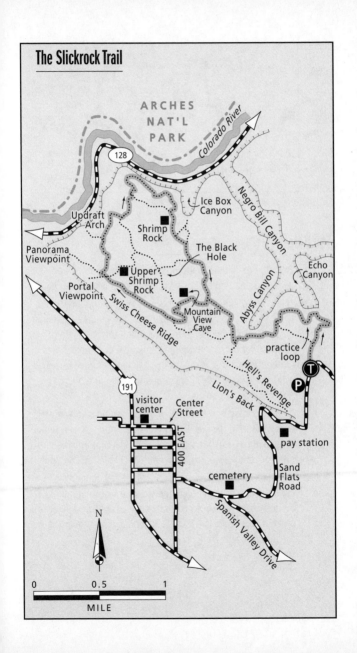

The Slickrock Trail

ARCHES NAT'L PARK

Colorado River

128

Updraft Arch

Ice Box Canyon

Shrimp Rock

The Black Hole

Negro Bill Canyon

Panorama Viewpoint

Portal Viewpoint

Upper Shrimp Rock

Swiss Cheese Ridge

Mountain View Cave

Abyss Canyon

Echo Canyon

practice loop

P T

191

visitor center

Center Street

400 EAST

Hell's Revenge

Lion's Back

pay station

cemetery

Sand Flats Road

Spanish Valley Drive

N

0   0.5   1

MILE

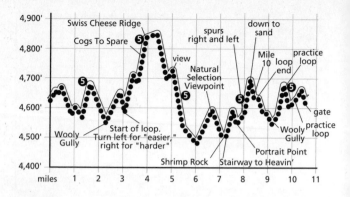

4,900'
Swiss Cheese Ridge
Cogs To Spare
spurs
right and left
down to
sand
4,800'
Mile practice
10 loop loop
view
end
Natural
Selection
Viewpoint
4,700'
4,600'
gate
Wooly
Gully
Start of loop.
Turn left for "easier,"
right for "harder"
Wooly practice
Gully loop
4,500'
Portrait Point
Shrimp Rock Stairway to Heavin'
4,400'
miles   1   2   3   4   5   6   7   8   9   10   11

The Ride

0.0 From the parking lot head north to the well-marked trail-head. Odometer readings start at the mini-cattleguard gate.

0.2 This first hill foreshadows the ride's delights and arrives at the first decision point. Turn right onto the practice loop. It is no easier than the rest of the trail, but it offers a taste of slickrock for those without time, strength, or desire to ride the entire trail. It also makes the trail longer for those who want more rock! A left here heads 0.8 mile to the junction described as 1.6 below.

0.7 A spur goes right to Echo Point. Spurs are marked with white dots instead of dashes. Be careful when going to viewpoints! They tend to be located on very high cliffs that appear suddenly. (Odometer readings do not reflect side trips on spurs.)

1.6 The practice loop merges with the Main Trail. Keep right to continue or left to complete the practice loop and return to the trailhead. By now you've gauged your skills and fitness to make a good decision. It's 0.8 mile back to the trailhead. If you're ready, let's go right.

2.1 The Abyss viewpoint.

2.2 The dashes descend into a wash to what is probably the hairiest move so far: a rough, ledgy drop into a sandy gully immediately followed by a rock hop back onto the sandstone. Locals call this Wooly Gully. Oh, what fun it is! A spur leaves to the left just prior to the wash heading to the Hell's Revenge Jeep Trail.

2.3 This sand trap precedes a spur left that cuts to the 3.7-mile point and accesses a sandy route beneath Swiss Cheese Ridge. To exit the trap requires a deft technically challenging move and good line selection. Some riders' cheeks may hurt by now from all the grinning! There's plenty more ahead!

2.9 Join the main loop! EASIER and HARDER are painted on the rock at this intersection. This description opts for the clockwise—easier—direction. See Highlights and the elevation profile for why.

3.5 Mountain View Cave comes into sight (to the right) up on the rock. Then a spur to The Black Hole goes right.

3.7 The spur from mile 2.3 reenters on the left. Don't look now, but a rock wall blocks the path ahead! It's the hill mentioned in the Highlights. To have any chance of climbing Cogs To Spare, hit the lower part with some speed and clean a grooved section of rock while nailing the granny gear. "All" that remains is the incredibly steep climb up to Swiss Cheese Ridge—most mortals will dismount and push this one. The top is a welcome level grade.

4.3 Before the main trail turns right and leaves Swiss Cheese Ridge, look left to see Moab, Moab Rim, Gold Bar Rim, and The Portal. The Portal is where the Colorado River crosses the Moab fault and heads into Canyonlands National Park. It is also where the famous and dangerous Portal Trail runs (see Ride 31). A spur continues ahead to the Portal Viewpoint.

4.35 Another spur goes right just after the first technical drop of the descent. It wanders past Upper Shrimp Rock and intersects with two other spurs.

4.4 The spur to Panorama Viewpoint darts left for some hair-raising vertical exposure!

4.7 Spin through a little sand to raise your appreciation for the smooth rock. A spur goes left to a cliffside view of the Colorado River below Updraft Arch.

5.4 A spur heads right to the three-way intersection below Upper Shrimp Rock.

6.1 A spur cuts right to a point 0.3 mile short of Shrimp Rock.

6.6 Natural Selection Viewpoint. Be careful near the edge to keep your DNA in the genetic pool.

6.8 The spur from mile 6.1 enters on the right.

7.1 Shrimp Rock. This may be the heart of Moab's mountain-biking soul. Speak your favorite mantra, and eat an energy bar to honor this holiest of rocks.

7.3 This steep, known as Stairway to Heavin', starts with a 3-foot rock hop.

7.6 This spur heads left to the Ice Box Canyon Viewpoint.

7.8 The Ice Box spur returns on the left.

7.9 Spurs head off right and left, marked by fake dinosaur tracks. Left is a sandy four-wheel-drive road, and right goes behind The Black Hole.

8.2 Drop down to some sand.

8.5 Back at the HARDER-EASIER junction. Go left to return to the trailhead.

9.8 Keep right for the direct route home. It's relatively level for 0.3 mile, then one last grunt. The Practice Loop leaves to the left here.

10.4 With the parking lot in sight, a sudden wheel-grabbing ditch sneaks up. "Matt's Mellon" lacks the telltale danger paint.

10.5 Trailhead.

10.6 Parking lot.

2 Klondike Bluffs

Location: 16 miles north of Moab.

Distance: 14.4-mile out-and-back.

Approximate riding time: 2 to 3 hours. Allow extra time to *hike* into Arches National Park for lunch.

Physical difficulty: Moderately easy. This is one of the easier rides in the region. The slickrock has some steeps, but the rest is pretty gradual.

Technical difficulty: Moderate. Most of the gravel road is easy to moderate. The four-wheel-drive road and slickrock portion are moderately difficult and are typically harder going down than up.

Trail surface: 5.6 miles on gravel road; 5.6 miles on four-wheel-drive road; 3.2 miles on slickrock. The four-wheel-drive road tickles the tires with rocks, erosion, and sand traps. The white slickrock is a bit lumpy.

Highlights: An excellent first ride offering slickrock, dinosaur tracks, and expansive views with only a little sand and steep. Klondike helps to shed light on your slickrock skills (possessed or needed). The hike (bikes are prohibited) at the end of the trail looks into Arches National Park and makes a great lunch spot.

Land status: State and BLM land bordering Arches National Park.

Maps: USGS Klondike Bluffs, Merrimac Butte (first 0.5 mile of route).

Finding the trailhead: The trailhead lies 17.3 miles north on U.S. Highway 191 from Center Street in Moab. After passing mile marker 142, continue 0.5 mile to the dirt road on the right signed for Klondike Bluffs (turn right just before a bridge's cement abutment). To access the alternate trailhead, follow the trail description 2.8 miles down the road.

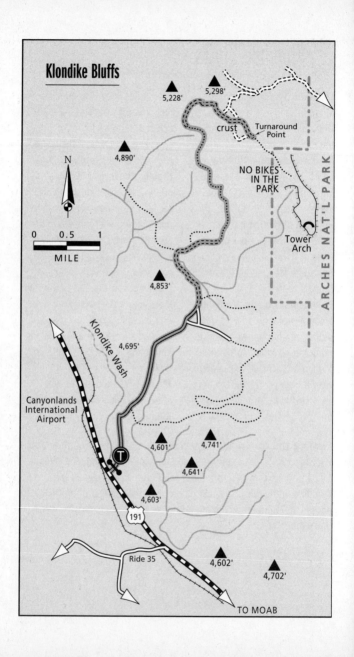

Klondike Bluffs

N

0   0.5   1
MILE

5,228'
5,298'
4,890'
crust
Turnaround Point

NO BIKES IN THE PARK

ARCHES NAT'L PARK

Tower Arch

4,853'

Klondike Wash
4,695'

Canyonlands International Airport

T

4,601'   4,741'
4,641'

4,603'

191

Ride 35   4,602'
4,702'

TO MOAB

The Ride

0.0 Pass through the gate and close it. Mount up and follow the gravel road north.

1.0 A spur goes right; stay left on the main road through the rolling hills. The patches of green dirt cast a surreal light on things.

2.5 Keep left through this intersection.

2.8 Second gate. This is the alternate trailhead. Pass through the gate and continue north on the road, which is now a four-wheel-drive track.

3.1 Sand trap! This is the first of two prominent sand traps. It's rideable, but getting off and pushing saves energy and equipment.

3.5 Sand trap number two.

3.6 The road forks; turn right. An arrow should point the way unless nature or bullets have destroyed the marker.

3.8 A spur goes left; stay right. Look for painted dinosaur track trail blazes on the rock. Cairns tend to be easier to spot, however.

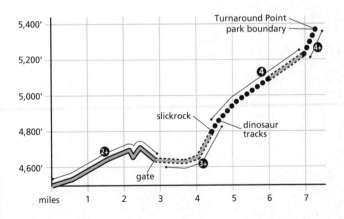

4.0 The road becomes rocky and eroded. Thread the rocks with your knobbies.

4.4 Begin the slickrock ascent. It is strenuous going for a bit.

4.5 Bear left, staying on the edge of the rock.

4.6 Start looking for real dinosaur tracks. The big ones are about 1 foot long and may be circled with rocks. A particularly nice set is preserved at the slickrock's edge as the route bears up to the right. They've been described as birdlike. Definitely not your average roadrunner!

4.9 Crank through a brief dirt section bearing left, then up the slickrock bearing right.

5.0 Be careful crossing the moderate-to-challenging dip on the slickrock to the right, then keep following cairns.

5.1 A huge cairn sits atop this viewpoint. The trail turns left and down briefly before turning right and up the slickrock. Missing the turn leads down the four-wheel-drive road and skips a wonderful section of slickrock.

6.1 Ignore the faint road that heads down the wash to stern. Stay on the main road. Note this spot to avoid a wrong turn on the way back.

6.3 The road forks; go right. Left leads over to Salt Valley.

6.6 Keep left. Right fizzles into a crypto-crust abuse situation.

6.9 Stay left to finish the ride by climbing technical singletrack. Right is a short trip to an abandoned mining site.

7.2 End of the line. Park your bike and hike up to see into Arches National Park. Stay right and walk up onto the slickrock. Cairns lead the way to a fabulous view of the Klondike Kliffs. Retrace the route home.

3 Courthouse Wash

Location: 6 miles north of Moab.
Distance: 25.9-mile loop or 16.1-mile one-way with a shuttle.
Approximate riding time: 3 to 6 hours.
Physical difficulty: Moderate but long. The paved climb in Arches National Park can be a heartbreaker because it comes late in the ride and traffic can be heavy.
Technical difficulty: Moderate. One section is challenging.
Trail surface: 16.1 miles on four-wheel-drive and singletrack; 9.8 miles on paved road. When wet the route is slick and best avoided.
Highlights: This tasty desert ride climbs among tall, red-rock cliffs, then skirts meringue-topped sandstone offering an up close look at arches with the La Sals as a backdrop. If 26 miles sounds too much like a marathon, consider doing a shuttle by leaving a vehicle in Arches National Park at the picnic area mentioned at mile 16.1 in the description. Seeing Arches by bike is a whole new experience. Be careful on paved roads—motorists tend to watch the scenery rather than the road. Arches charges an entry fee of $10/vehicle. Receipts are good for four days and an annual pass is $50.
Land status: BLM, state, and Arches National Park.
Maps: USGS Gold Bar Canyon, Merrimac Butte, The Windows Section, and Moab. The Moab and Gold Bar topos cover little of the route.

Finding the trailhead: From Center Street in Moab drive 5 miles north on U.S. Highway 191 and pass the entrance to Arches National Park. Continue 0.6 mile to a gravel parking area on the right. To leave a shuttle vehicle in the park, turn in at the main entrance and drive about 9 miles north on the main park road. Turn left at Balanced Rock onto Willow Springs Road and park at the picnic area mentioned at mile 16.1 in the description.

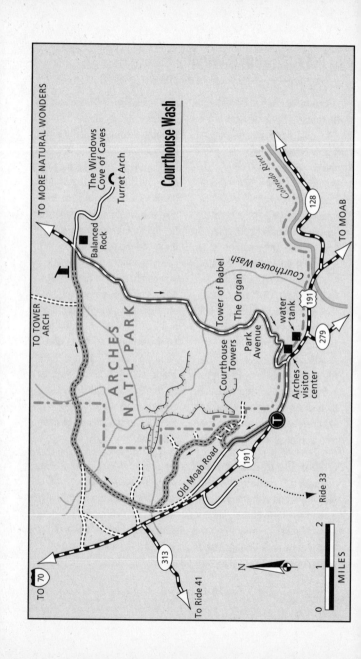

Courthouse Wash

TO MORE NATURAL WONDERS

The Windows
Cove of Caves
Turret Arch

Balanced Rock

TO TOWER ARCH

ARCHES NAT'L PARK

Tower of Babel
The Organ
Courthouse Wash

Courthouse Towers

Park Avenue

water tank

Arches visitor center

Old Moab Road

191

313

TO 70

To Ride 41

Ride 33

279

191

128

Colorado River

TO MOAB

N

MILES
0   1   2

The Ride

0.0 Start up the old highway on the left side of the parking area and cross the old bridge.

2.6 The road turns to dirt. Turn onto the first road to the right. It's possible to stay straight here and take Old Moab Road to Willow Springs Road and rejoin the route at the 10.2 mark.

2.8 Turn right. A whole myriad of choices start to show up. No worries—they all tend to deposit you on route.

3.0 Keep right at this three-way fork.

3.3 The road bears right and crosses a boulder patch (moderate to challenging).

3.4 Turn right at this four-way junction and rejoin the road that was the middle route at mile 3.

3.9 Turn left here—almost a U-turn. Right heads to a nice view spot. The route now heads north with some spectacular slickrock on the right. Watch for the park boundary if you explore!

4.4 Keep right on the road that lies straight ahead.

4.5 Stay right through this old party site and watch for glass.

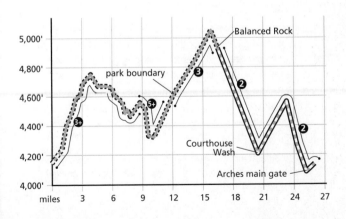

4.8 Keep on the main road through these spurs.

5.1 The main route doesn't descend this rocky road. Instead, go left before the downhill. (But downhill does lead 0.2 mile to a view across a huge meringue of white and orange rock with the La Sals looming over the dish and Arches National Park waiting for a serving.)

5.7 Stay left as another spur to a viewpoint goes right (0.8 mile to more dessert for the eyes).

6.2 Stay on the main road as yet another road joins from the left.

6.9 An obscure track goes left to the hilltop. Keep straight.

7.2 Drop into the wash and turn right.

7.3 Go left and out of the wash.

7.4 Follow singletrack to the left. This skinny trail is moderate to challenging.

7.5 Turn right onto "pipeline road," which is marked by orange signs. Stay on this road, ignoring all spurs.

7.7 Cross the wash . . . then a sandy stretch . . . then a steep pitch.

8.0 A road joins from the right. Stay straight.

8.2 Cross through a four-way intersection following the pipeline road.

9.3 As the road turns left to avoid a dropoff, look for a faint trail going right. Cairns mark the way. This trail eventually returns to the pipeline road after a challenging descent that will have you hoping your insurance is paid up.

9.9 Ride along the wash, then cross it after passing a cement block on the opposite bank. Take either the trail at the cement block or the road that restarts slightly farther down the wash.

10.2 Turn right onto Willow Springs Road. A gas company structure marks the intersection. Keep right, away from the pipeline road.

10.8 Stay right.

11.4 Stay right.

11.6 Turn left—*not* up the steep, eroded doubletrack.

12.1 Arches National Park boundary.

12.9 Sandy tread makes this climb harder than expected—or maybe it's time for a snack.

15.4 Stay straight (right) as a four-wheel-drive road goes left to Eye of the Whale and Tower Arch.

16.1 Pass through this picnic area complete with bathroom. (This is a good place to be dropped off to ride this route in reverse and meet your ride at the entrance station.)

16.2 Balanced Rock. When done with your gawk at the rawk, turn right onto the paved main park road. (Left leads deeper into Arches.)

20.4 The downhill ends here at Courthouse Wash. Ahead and on the left is the Tower of Babel followed by The Organ. That's Three Gossips on the right.

23.3 Park Avenue rolls by on the right—pass go and start a kamikaze descent.

25.2 Arches main gate.

25.3 Turn right onto US 191 and pedal north to the parking area.

25.9 Court adjourned.

4 Pole Canyon Rim

Location: 33 miles northeast of Moab.

Distance: 12.1-mile out-and-back.

Approximate riding time: 2 hours.

Physical difficulty: Strenuous. The initial climb is grueling, but once on top the ride becomes much easier.

Technical difficulty: Moderate to challenging. The actual obstacles aren't that bad. The trouble stems from the steeps that the obstacles are on.

Trail surface: 2.4 miles on gravel road; 9.7 miles on four-wheel-drive roads. The four-wheel-drive portions consist of broken and loose rock on a packed surface. Once up on the rim, soft patches become common.

Highlights: Looking down on the Colorado River and boaters going by gives a king-of-the-hill feeling. But be careful—watching the power lines descend into the valley induces vertigo. The best biking part of this trip is the downhill, which is uncrowded and fast. The climb is shorter and easier than Top of the World (Ride 5), but the view, while spectacular, isn't as far-reaching.

Land status: BLM.

Map: USGS Dewey.

Finding the trailhead: From Center and Main in Moab, drive 2.6 miles north on U.S. Highway 191. Turn right onto Utah Highway 128, and drive 30.8 miles northeast to the Dewey recreation site, complete with outhouses. Go another 0.2 mile, and look for a right-hand turn in the middle of a curve. It's easy to miss as you prepare to cross the Colorado River. Turn right here, and park by the old Dewey Bridge.

The Ride

0.0 From Dewey Bridge, head up the dirt road.

0.3 Keep on the main road as a spur goes left.

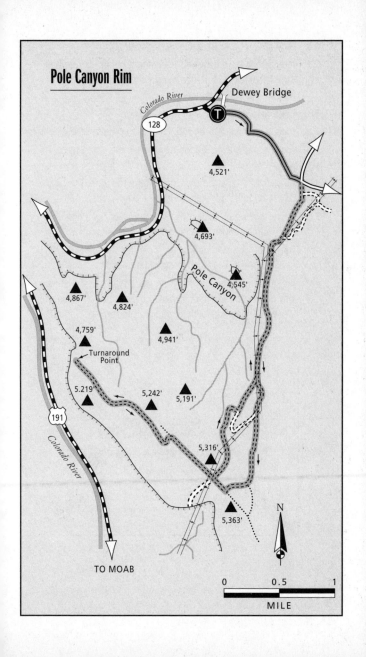

Pole Canyon Rim

Colorado River

128

Dewey Bridge

T

4,521'

4,693'

4,545'

Pole Canyon

4,867'

4,824'

4,941'

4,759'

Turnaround
Point

5,219'

5,242'

5,191'

191

Colorado River

5,316'

5,363'

N

TO MOAB

0   0.5   1
MILE

0.8 Stay on the main road as a spur goes right.

1.2 Intersection. Turn right and begin the grunt up to Pole Canyon Rim. The track is immediately technical and steep but becomes a bit more gradual.

1.7 Keep right as a road joins from the left.

1.9 Pass a spur going right and follow the power lines up the hill.

2.8 A cairn marks a right-hand turn. This is the return route. For now, bear left.

3.0 Keep right then left as two spurs leave the road. The second one is an optional return route.

3.8 A slickrock patch marks this right turn. Missing it simply adds some sandy mileage to the total.

4.0 Up on top. An extremely sandy lookout point lies straight ahead but is best avoided. Instead, turn right.

4.2 Important intersection! The road going right is the eventual way home, and left runs less than 0.5 mile to an electrifying viewpoint. Instead, continue straight (northwest).

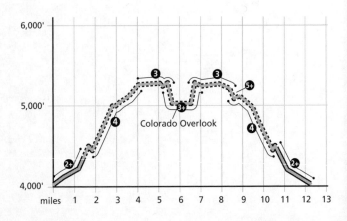

5.0 The road turns back on itself and heads over a ridge. A dead-end spur goes right.

6.0 After a technical descent and a quick slickrock snack, the road ends at a cliff overlooking the Colorado River 1,040 feet below. When you've had your fill of scenery, retrace the route to the important intersection at mile 4.2 above.

7.8 Turn left at the intersection.

8.2 Bear left where the power lines dive off the cliff. The road drops down an insanely steep, loose, and ledgy slope, then turns right.

8.3 Turn left here and zoom downhill (right loops south and east to also reconnect with the main road, but it's longer).

8.7 Turn left and retrace the route home.

12.1 Dewey Bridge and the trailhead.

5 Top of the World

Location: 33 miles northeast of Moab.

Distance: 18.8-mile out-and-back; 8.6 miles if riding from the alternate trailhead.

Approximate riding time: 3 hours; 1.5 hours from the alternate trailhead.

Physical difficulty: Strenuous. The climb alone is steep. Pair that with the technical nature of the trail, and the result is rubber legs and aching lungs.

Technical difficulty: Moderate to challenging. The obstacles are frequent and occur on steeps requiring good rubber-legged, rock-hopping abilities.

Trail surface: 10.2 miles on gravel road; 8.4 miles on four-wheel-drive road. The four-wheel-drive road consists of broken slickrock, packed dirt, and slickrock proper.

Highlights: Sing along with Karen: "I'm on the . . . Top of the World looking . . . down on creation . . . ." and the only explanation I can find is that, as tough as this trail is physically, its beauty is worth the trip. The Mystery and Titan Towers jut up from below; the La Sals rise to the south; and the rock formations— Coffee Pot, Covenant, Mother Superior, Priest and Nuns, and the tip of Castle Rock—are all visible. On a clear day you can see into Colorado and the highlands to the north. Parriott Mesa and Arches National Park are also in sight.

Land status: BLM.

Maps: USGS Dewey, Blue Chief Mesa, Fisher Towers.

Finding the trailhead: From Center and Main in Moab, drive 2.6 miles north on U.S. Highway 191. Turn right onto Utah Highway 128. Pass by Matrimony Springs (see the section on water in the Introduction). About 33.6 miles from Center Street, turn right on a dirt road that leaves the highway in the middle of a curve. It's tough to see— the gap in the guardrail is slim. (If you miss it, you'll immediately run

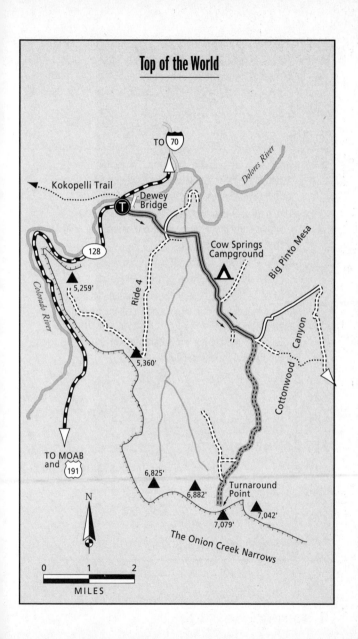

Top of the World

Kokopelli Trail

Dewey Bridge

TO 70

Dolores River

128

Cow Springs Campground

Big Pinto Mesa

Colorado River

5,259'

Ride 4

5,360'

Cottonwood Canyon

TO MOAB and 191

6,825'

6,882'

Turnaround Point

7,079'

7,042'

The Onion Creek Narrows

N

0   1   2

MILES

onto the modern version of Dewey Bridge spanning the Colorado River.) Park in the area provided next to the old Dewey Bridge. If the road has recently been graded, however, a family car can make it down the washboarded road an additional 5.1 miles to the alternate trailhead.

The Ride

0.0 Head southeast up the gravel road, away from Dewey Bridge. Avoid all spurs for 5.1 miles. The road rolls up and down before settling into a constant climb.

3.4 The road passes a couple of slickrock playgrounds, then Cowskin Campground comes up on the left. The road turns right and grows steeper.

4.5 A spur goes right. No matter how much you wish for this to be the route, it's not. Keep on the main road.

5.1 A backroad junction marks the alternate trailhead. The gravel road bends left and then goes downhill. Instead, turn right onto the four-wheel-drive road and keep right. The four-wheel-drive road going left is part of Dolores River Overlook, (Ride 6) and the Kokopelli Trail (Ride 42).

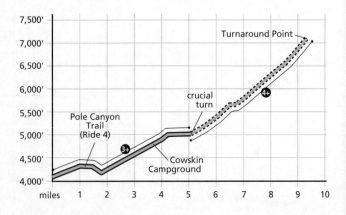

5.3 Leave the gate as is.

5.4 Begin a 0.3-mile slickrock ascent.

5.8 Stay left as a spur heads right. Yup, keep climbing. Looking down makes it seem less steep.

6.8 Bear right as a faint old road continues ahead.

7.1 Surprise! The climb eases for a rare break.

7.4 Back into the climb and it's getting more technical.

8.1 Stay left on the slickrock as a faint road leaves to the right.

8.4 At a fork in the road marked with a cairn, veer right and up broken slickrock. This is the final stretch.

9.4 *Stop!!!* The slickrock ahead goes straight to the cliff's edge, then drops about 2,400 feet. After the long climb the stupendous vistas are a welcome excuse to take a rest. When your soul is full, turn around and follow your tire tracks for the white-knuckle descent to the trailhead.

6 Dolores River Overlook

Location: 38 miles east of Moab.

Distance: 20-mile out-and-back, or 30.2-mile round-trip from Dewey Bridge.

Approximate riding time: 2 to 4 hours.

Physical difficulty: Strenuous. The climbs are long; seek a sustained grunting groove.

Technical difficulty: Moderate to challenging. Cottonwood Canyon and the drop toward the Dolores River contain lots of erosional hazards. The grind between is comparatively smooth.

Trail surface: 5 miles on gravel road; 15 miles on four-wheel-drive road. In places the four-wheel-drive road is rutted, with exposed, loose rocks. Sections of the gravel road may have washboards.

Highlights: The initial drop into Cottonwood Canyon is twisty, steep, and rugged. In other words: fun, fun, and more fun. Then a long, steady climb leads to a lactic-acid flushing downhill to the overlook of the Dolores River in its canyon. Don't let thoughts of the climb back home spoil the scenery—those same long grades keep traffic here to a minimum, a welcome respite from Moab's fat-tire parades.

Land status: BLM.

Maps: USGS Blue Chief Mesa, Fisher Valley.

Finding the trailhead: From Center and Main in Moab, drive 2.6 miles north on U.S. Highway 191. Turn right onto Utah Highway 128, and drive 31 miles northeast. Turn right onto a dirt road that leaves Utah 128 in the middle of a turn. This side road is hard to see because the gap in the guardrail is short. Park here if the road ahead looks too rough. If the road has been recently graded, continue 5.1 miles to the trailhead. Set your odometer and watch for the parking area, which comes up after two spurs on the right. The main road bends left and drops downhill. Park where two more spurs go right from the main road.

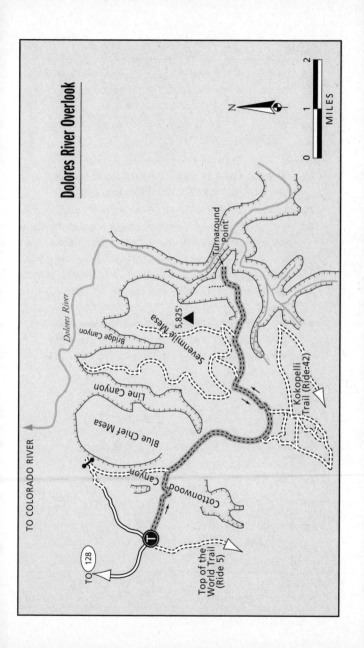

Dolores River Overlook

TO COLORADO RIVER

TO 128

Dolores River

Bridge Canyon

Blue Chief Mesa

Line Canyon

Sevenmile Mesa

5,825'

Turnaround Point

Cottonwood Canyon

Kokopelli Trail (Ride 42)

Top of the World Trail (Ride 5)

N

0   1   2
MILES

The Ride

0.0 Two four-wheel-drive spurs leave the parking area, one heading south and the other east. Take the eastbound track (the road south goes to Top of the World—see Ride 5).

1.0 The road continues its rough, wild ride as it snakes down into Cottonwood Canyon.

1.5 The short climb back out of the canyon starts here.

2.2 The road joins an offshoot of the main access road. Turn right and find your favorite gear for the long climb ahead.

4.3 A spur climbs away right; stay left on the main road.

4.7 Turn left at this fork as the main road continues down to the Kokopelli Trail (and into a second Cottonwood Canyon.)

5.5 After a few ups and downs, the road tops out. From here it's all downhill to the Dolores River Overlook. Stay on the main road, ignoring all spurs. The road forks at about mile 9.5— stay left.

10.0 Roll up to the Dolores River Overlook, and enjoy a well-earned rest. You'll need it for the initial climb out on the return leg. Turn around and retrace your tracks back to the trailhead.

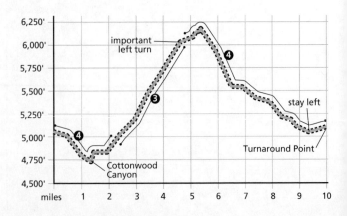

7 Onion Creek

Location: 35 miles east of Moab.

Distance: 26.2-mile one-way.

Approximate riding time: 3 hours (plus a long shuttle).

Physical difficulty: Moderate. A great deal of the workout will be upper body. There is one nasty hill that begins at mile 14.3.

Technical difficulty: Moderate. Speed, creek crossings, and erosion will make your eyes water. Or is it the onions?

Trail surface: 26.2 miles on four-wheel-drive road. When wet the route is slick and best avoided. The route crosses Onion Creek countless times, making for a wet and wild ride. It's no use trying to keep dry.

Highlights: Riding in a twisted landscape of deep reds and strange whites is otherworldly. No wonder movies are shot in this area so often. Picture John Wayne riding his steed down, down, and farther down from the mesa tops to the bottoms in Professor Valley. One major uphill slaps riders in the face at mile 14.3. The only real problem with the ride is the extreme shuttle, but it's worth it! Bring a towel and a dry set of clothes to keep the inside of your cars clean. *Caution:* Don't ride this if there is a chance of flooding. Getting caught in the narrows in a flood will carry you downstream in a manner that the human body was not designed for.

Land status: Manti–La Sal National Forest, BLM, and private holdings.

Maps: USGS Mount Waas, Fisher Valley, Fisher Towers.

Finding the trailhead: First drop off a shuttle vehicle at the ride's end. From Moab drive 2.6 miles north on U.S. Highway 191 to Utah Highway 128. Turn right, and drive 22 miles northeast to Onion Creek Road (passing Castleton Road on the right 16.1 miles from US 191—the road to the trailhead). Park the shuttle car at the parking area 0.7 mile down the Onion Creek Road. Now backtrack 5.9 miles south on Utah 128, and turn left onto Castleton Road. Drive 11 miles south

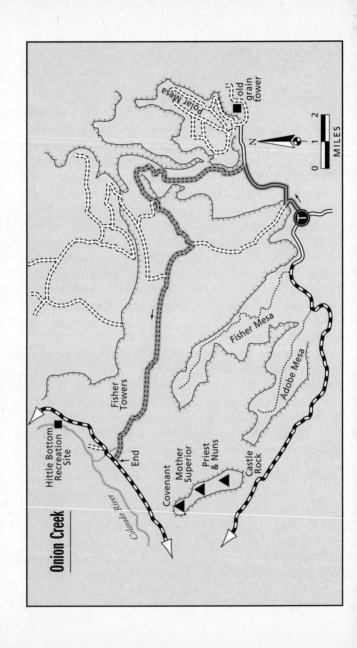

Onion Creek

Colorado River

Hittle Bottom Recreation Site

End

Fisher Towers

Covenant

Mother Superior

Priest & Nuns

Castle Rock

Fisher Mesa

Adobe Mesa

Polar Mesa

old grain tower

T

N

0   1   2
MILES

and turn left (the paved Loop Road goes right and south). Go 8 miles east (the road turns to gravel), and park at the junction with Forest Road 033.

The Ride

0.0 Roll northeast on FR 033, which heads downhill and passes a corral.

0.5 An obscure ATV route goes left. This is a savage shortcut portage into Fisher Valley. Instead, stay on the main road, which road climbs a short hill.

4.3 In the middle of this downhill run, turn left at the easy-to-miss Kokopelli Trail marker. Straight continues on to Polar Mesa. Stay left on this road past the two spurs that show up in the next 2 miles. Don't grow numb to the scenery. This ride is just beginning!

7.3 The road bends sharply left. A shortcut goes right, but left leads to a stunning view of Onion Creek Narrows to the west, past an offshoot of Hideout Canyon.

14.3 A killer hill. Didn't believe me, huh?

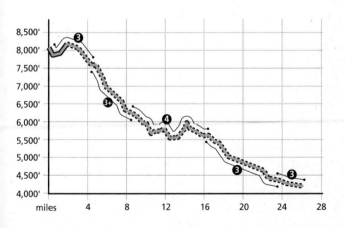

15.2 Go right as the road forks. Left runs south about 8 miles back to FR 033 and your car. But you'll have to carry your bike up the mesa rim to rejoin the road. And a big chunk of the fun is still ahead.

16.2 Turn left off the Kokopelli Trail. The Kokopelli heads back up Fisher Creek's Cottonwood Canyon.

16.7 Keep right here. Into the Onion Creek drainage we go like lemmings sucked into a whirlpool.

19.8 Can you smell Stinking Spring? The road is deep in the narrows now, and it's not done with the crossings!

21.2 The foot trail on the right climbs out of the canyon to grant a view of Fisher Towers.

24.7 Keep it pointed downhill as a road enters on the right.

26.2 Draw straws to go get the shuttle car. To wash up in the Colorado, head right up Utah 128. A spur left grants riverside access.

8 Polar Mesa

Location: 35 miles east of Moab.

Distance: 19-mile lariat-shaped loop.

Approximate riding time: 2 to 3 hours.

Physical difficulty: Moderate. There are two pretty good grunts, and the return is gradually uphill the whole way. It can be shortened dramatically using the alternative trailhead.

Technical difficulty: Moderate. Occasional soft patches and ruts are the main obstacles.

Trail surface: 11.4 miles on gravel road; 7.6 miles on four-wheel-drive road. The gravel road can be gooey when wet, and the four-wheel-drive tread tends to be overgrown and eroded.

Highlights: Some nice views of the La Sals and the plateau surrounding the Dolores River. An old mining rig complete with wrecked truck sits high up on the mesa. White rock here gives the area its name. The overgrown and rocky roads to the east are very hard to navigate but fun for the adventurous.

Land status: Manti–La Sal National Forest.

Maps: USGS Mount Waas, Fisher Valley.

Finding the trailhead: From Moab drive 2.6 miles north on U.S. Highway 191 to Utah Highway 128. Turn right, passing Matrimony Spring, and go 13 miles northeast. Turn right onto Castleton Road, drive 11 miles south, and turn left, remaining on Castleton Road (Forest Road 207. Note: The Loop Road heads right). Drive 8 miles to Forest Road 033. This is the first trailhead. Two alternate trailheads are 0.4 and 5.7 miles farther, as described below.

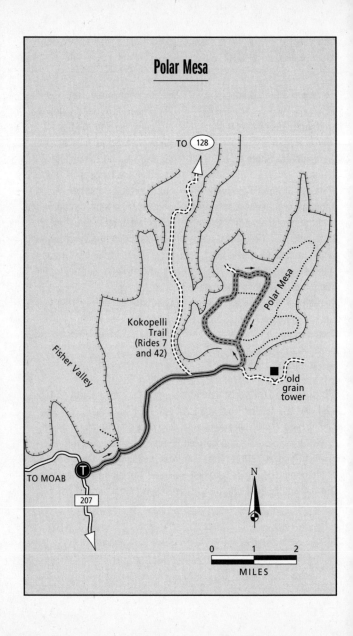

Polar Mesa

TO 128

Kokopelli Trail (Rides 7 and 42)

Fisher Valley

Polar Mesa

old grain tower

TO MOAB

207

N

0   1   2
MILES

The Ride

0.0 Head down FR 033. The stockade at 0.4 mile makes a good alternate trailhead to avoid a final steep climb on the return trip.

1.9 After a short grunt the road cruises along North Beaver Mesa.

4.4 Stay right. The Kokopelli Trail and Onion Creek Road leave to the left.

5.7 Stay left on the main road. This makes a good alternate trailhead to avoid the long, gradual climb upon return. A doubletrack to the right leads to a grain storage tower.

6.6 A cattleguard is near the end of this steep climb.

6.8 Turn left onto the initially technical Forest Road 610. This doubletrack gets a bit overgrown. Keep an eye out for hidden ruts and obstacles.

7.7 Keep right after crossing a meadow (Forest Road 611 goes left).

8.3 Remain on the main road as faint spurs head off. The spurs make for fun exploring, but they aren't part of the "official" route. This road is now labeled Forest Road 601. Go figure.

9.0 Pass by an old mine. The road gets pretty rutty here (technically moderate to challenging).

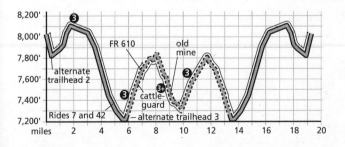

9.2 Turn right onto a well-groomed road. This road loops back to the trailhead.

11.8 Keep right as Forest Road 616 goes left. FR 616 is actually the return of an earlier spur, but that route is extremely tough to navigate.

12.2 Been here. Done that. FR 610 goes right. Instead, retrace the route going left to the car.

13.3 Alternate trailhead 3.

18.6 Alternate trailhead 2.

19.0 Trailhead.

9 Fisher Mesa

Location: 25 miles northeast of Moab on the La Sal Loop Road.
Distance: 20.8-mile out-and-back.
Approximate riding time: 3 hours.
Physical difficulty: Strenuous. This ride is tougher than it looks on the elevation profile. Yes, there's a lot of downhill on the way out, dropping about 1,500 feet in elevation, but this is punctuated by a handful of climbs. And the return trip gains back every inch of the 1,500 feet.
Technical difficulty: Moderate to challenging. The initial downhill is bouncy, and the climb up to Fisher Peak is on broken ground. The parts between are moderate.

Trail surface: 20.8 miles on four-wheel-drive road that includes packed dirt, eroded and rock-strewn sections, sand, and slickrock.
Highlights: The view of Professor Valley, Arches National Park, Castle Valley, and the Fisher Towers is clouded only by the nagging knowledge that the return climb awaits. The mesa-top ecosystem here is relatively unspoiled and definitely uncrowded. Well worth the effort. A new singletrack trail is being blazed on Fisher Mesa. Look for it to skirt the mesa's edges.
Land status: Manti–La Sal National Forest and BLM.
Maps: USGS Mount Waas, Fisher Valley, Fisher Towers.

Finding the trailhead: From Moab drive 2.6 miles north on U.S. Highway 191 to Utah Highway 128. Turn right, passing Matrimony Spring, and go 13 miles northeast. Turn right onto Castleton Road, drive 11 miles south, and turn left, remaining on Castleton Road (the Loop Road heads right). Drive 5.3 miles east, and look for Forest Road 601 on the left just before a cattleguard. It's easy to miss; if Castleton Road turns to dirt, you've gone 0.4 mile too far. High-clearance vehicles can turn left onto FR 601 and park in the camping area. The rest of us should park across the road among the tall ponderosa pines.

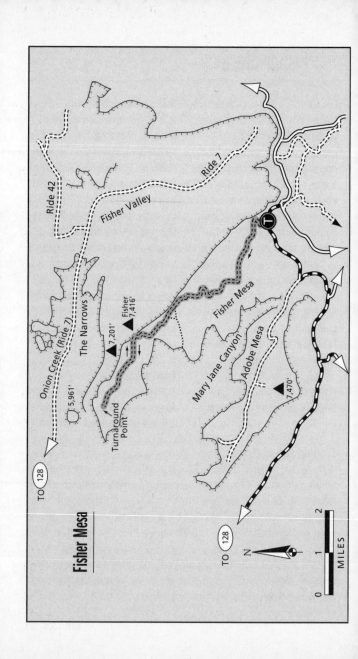

Fisher Mesa

TO (128)

Onion Creek (Ride 7)

Ride 42

Ride 7

Fisher Valley

The Narrows

5,961'

7,201'

Fisher
7,416'

T

Fisher Mesa

Mary Jane Canyon

Adobe Mesa

7,470'

Turnaround
Point

TO (128)

N

MILES

0   1   2

The Ride

0.0 Head north and downhill on FR 601 and immediately turn left.

0.2 Turn left at this fork. Numerous faint roads riddle this area. Simply stay left. Pass to the left of the outhouse.

0.3 A sweeping right-hand turn by a fence starts the dive down onto Fisher Mesa. Yehaaa!!

2.4 Pass by this sometimes-full-but-often-empty pond.

2.7 Stay left as Forest Road 602 goes right.

3.2 Bermed downhill! Beware deep ruts that can swallow you whole.

4.1 That's Mary Jane Canyon off to the left. I don't know how it got its name—but it's on all the maps.

4.4 Rock obstacles become more frequent. Here's one for your viewing pleasure that rates a technical difficulty of moderate to challenging.

4.6 Take the left fork up the marshmallow-less, rocky road (at least it's fat free).

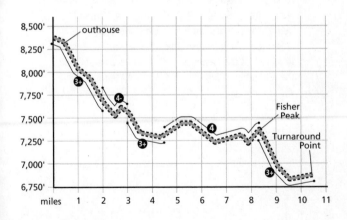

4.9 Roll through a forest of fire-killed trees. Before political correctness these were called burnt trees.

5.2 Another technical ascent. The road is faint here on the rock, but it soon becomes more evident.

5.4 The road breaks out on top for views of Adobe Mesa, Porcupine Rim, and the La Sals. Stay on the main road. The spurs, if you see them, head off to view Mary Jane Canyon.

6.3 After descending a brief switchback, keep left and below a large rock embankment. An old shed, about 100 yards uphill on the right, is not on the trail.

6.9 Awesome view to the right of Onion Creek Narrows and Fisher Valley as the route nears the mesa's edge.

7.1 Grunt up a short, steep, loose section that skirts a high, wide ledge, then contour on the slickrock to pick up the cairns marking the road.

7.2 More loose rock climbing.

7.9 More killer views. Avoid the cryptobiotic crust and have a look.

10.4 The last stretch is sandy, but the payoff point has arrived. The rock formations from left to right are Castle Rock, Priest and Nuns, Mother Superior, and the Covenant. Parriott Mesa lies behind the catholic rocks, and the Fisher Towers are the spires to the right across Onion Creek Narrows. Enjoy. Keep in mind that the obstacles will present a different face on the return trip to the trailhead. Retrace the route home.

20.8 Back at the car.

10 Adobe Mesa

Location: 28 miles northeast of Moab.

Distance: 11.6-mile out-and-back.

Approximate riding time: 2 to 4 hours.

Physical difficulty: Strenuous. Two extended climbs on the return trip leave legs aching. The climb out is a true test of will. It would certainly be nice to have the trailhead on the other end.

Technical difficulty: Moderate. A pretty straightforward ride with the main obstacles being ruts and rocks. Occasional sand patches keep things interesting.

Trail surface: 11.6 miles on four-wheel-drive road.

Highlights: Hellroaring and Mary Jane Canyons' dizzying drainages lie below this ride's terminus. The colors flow from brown to orange to reddish purple, contrasted with the green of Professor Valley framed by Fisher Mesa on the right. Views of Covenant and Mother Superior are great. Unfortunately the left-hand spur never delivers on the Castle Rock views, but Coffee Pot Rock and Porcupine Rim can be seen. If you hike, *please* find an all-slickrock, non-cryptobiotic route.

Land status: Manti–La Sal National Forest and BLM.

Maps: USGS Warner Lake, Fisher Towers.

Finding the trailhead: From Center Street in Moab, take U.S. Highway 191 north to Utah Highway 128, and turn right. Turn right onto Castleton Road at mile 16.1, and head through Castle Valley. Where the Loop Road joins, 11 miles from the highway, turn left onto Castleton Road and travel 3.3 miles. A Volkswagen-size boulder sits on the left side of the road next to two four-wheel- rive roads, marking the trailhead.

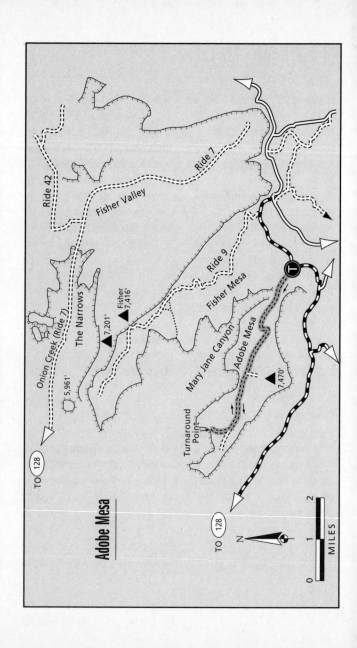

Adobe Mesa

TO 128

Ride 42

Onion Creek (Ride 7)

Fisher Valley

Ride 7

The Narrows

5,961'

▲ 7,201'

Fisher
▲ 7,416'

Ride 9

Fisher Mesa

Mary Jane Canyon

Adobe Mesa

▲ 7,470'

Turnaround
Point

TO 128

T

N

0   1   2
MILES

The Ride

0.0 Take the right-hand road downhill. The road to the left summits the small hill and ends.

1.0 This sandy hairpin can be tricky. It marks the end of the eroded, rocky downhill.

1.4 Pass through the gate, leaving it as it was.

2.3 Nice views of the La Sals and Porcupine Rim. A gnarly rock formation lies below this loose, cobblestone descent (rated at moderate to challenging).

4.7 The road forks; stay left.

4.8 The road forks again; stay right. Left goes to a fun little slickrock play area.

5.3 Intersection; continue straight. Left offers an extremely sandy approach toward the mesa's edge, but it never quite gets there.

5.8 Don't do a Chevy Chase at this overlook. Absorb the vertigo-inducing view of the Onion Creek drainage before turning around to retrace the route back to your vehicle.

11.6 Trailhead.

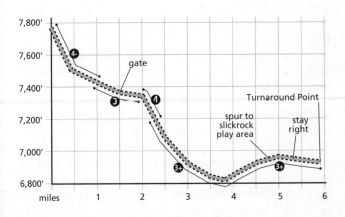

11 Bachelor's Bash

Location: 25 miles east of Moab off the La Sal Loop Road.

Distance: 15.9-mile loop.

Approximate riding time: 3 to 5 hours.

Physical difficulty: Strenuous. If you don't like gut-wrenching climbs or won't push your bike up one, then think twice about tackling this ride.

Technical difficulty: Moderate to challenging. A few stretches are definitely challenging and, if the winter downed a lot of trees, the singletrack may be tougher. The sheer steepness of the ride is an obstacle in itself.

Trail surface: 4.9 miles on singletrack and doubletrack; 4.8 miles on four-wheel-drive road; 6.2 miles on paved road. The four-wheel-drive road is packed dirt with some loose rocks sprinkled on top for flavor. The singletrack and doubletrack are packed dirt covered with leaves and pine needles. Downfall is plentiful in Bachelor's Basin.

Highlights: The descent into Bachelor Basin is sweet! It weaves through a high-altitude forest and features some tantalizing technical sections. The climb up Miner's Basin is intense and offers vistas of the Canyon Country below. Most riders stop and admire the view—often. In August a deer grazed in the flower-filled meadow at mile 3, and trout were visible in the crystal-clear lake. This route has long, uphill struggles and rapid races downhill—the joys of bachelorhood.

Land status: Manti–La Sal National Forest.

Maps: USGS Warner Lake, Mount Waas.

Finding the trailhead: From Center Street in Moab, take U.S. Highway 191 north to Utah Highway 128, and turn right. Go to mile 16.1, turn right onto Castleton Road, and head through Castle Valley. Go 11 miles from the highway, and turn right onto the Loop Road. It's 6.2 more miles to the trailhead. A sign on the mountain side of the road marks Miner's Basin, and on the other side of the road one

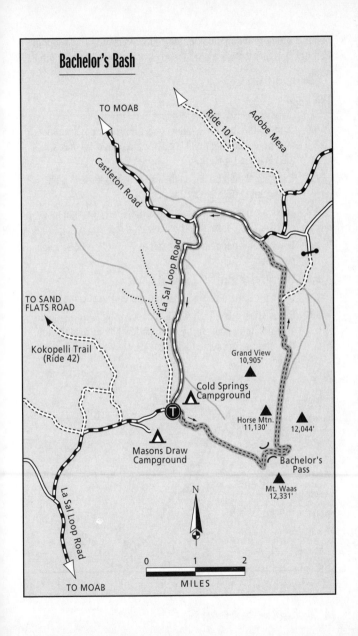

Bachelor's Bash

TO MOAB

Ride 10

Adobe Mesa

Castleton Road

La Sal Loop Road

TO SAND
FLATS ROAD

Kokopelli Trail
(Ride 42)

Grand View
10,905'

Cold Springs
Campground

Horse Mtn.
11,130'

12,044'

Masons Draw
Campground

Bachelor's
Pass

La Sal Loop Road

Mt. Waas
12,331'

N

0   1   2
MILES

TO MOAB

points the way to the Pinhook Battleground. Park in the Cold Springs Campground, just before the trailhead on the mountain side of the road.

The Ride

0.0 Start up the four-wheel-drive road. I do mean up. If you need a warm-up, consider parking down the road a few miles (see the elevation profile).

1.1 This gate should be left as found. The grade lessens a bit after gaining 650 feet to this point.

2.8 Cross a cattleguard. The road forks; stay left (the right fork ganders at the lake, then heads up the meadow).

3.0 The meadow ends here. Keep left as Forest Road 681 peels away right.

3.3 Stay right, passing the caretaker's cabins.

3.4 Cross the stream(s), and bow into more serious climbing.

3.5 This section gets a tech rating of challenging. It mellows into a moderate-to-challenging ride with few breaks until the top. The road passes some ruined cabins. Look but please don't touch.

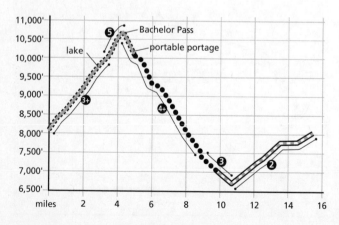

4.2 Top! You now have a choice to make. Straight ahead is a gentler initial descent that later requires a brief portage. An immediate left 40 yards down the road is steeper and very technical, but also 0.4 mile shorter. (For those who go left: The road switchbacks sharply down the rocky shale slope. If the trail disappears, look behind you for another switchback. Rejoin the rest of us at mile 4.9 in the description below.) Everybody else, go straight.

4.4 After some brief technically moderate-to-challenging rock gardens, keep left. The right-hand fork offers outstanding views of Bachelor Basin's rock spires.

4.6 Turn left here, just up from a rusty piece of mining hardware.

4.8 After passing the ruined bachelor pads, the trail is blocked by downfall. Portage around this, keeping to the left. A tree with a sign that says TRAIL is the goal. Portaging too far left leads to a roadbed. Take the road down and to the right. Don't portage to the right.

4.9 A Trail sign points the way. Also watch for a cairn here. Faint singletrack continues to be marked with cairn and blazes on the trees. Simply follow the pinecone-strewn, brown ribbon of singletrack righteousness. Be alert for downfall and rocks that can come up rather suddenly.

5.9 The going is getting technical. Downfall blocks the way, then some tight switchbacks rear up. Plan on dismounting for more trees across the trail.

6.2 Watch for obstacles hiding under the grass as the singletrack officially becomes doubletrack.

6.9 Avoid the faint doubletrack spur to the left—it's a dead end.

7.0 Go left on faint singletrack. With any luck it should be marked with a cairn or a pile of wood. If not, and you still find the turn, please reassemble the marker. Continuing on the road will get you out, but only by trespassing. You're better off if you can find the singletrack.

9.7 The trail deltas out to a parking area. Turn left onto Castleton Road. This is a good place for a shuttle or alternate trail-head.

11.3 Turn left onto La Sal Loop Road. This leads all the way back to the trailhead.

13.2 Forest Road 628 disappears to the right. Stay on the paved road.

13.9 Admire the lone ponderosa, and ask it for strength to carry on.

15.9 Trailhead.

12 Burro Pass

Location: 28 miles east of Moab in the La Sal Mountains.
Distance: 11.4-mile loop.
Approximate riding time: 2.5 to 5 hours.
Physical difficulty: Strenuous. The climbs are steep, with the exception of some parts of Geyser Pass Road. Very few riders will summit Burro without pushing their mounts. The initial climb can be made more gradual (and longer) by starting at the base of Geyser Pass Road and returning via Oowah Lake Road and the La Sal Loop Road.
Technical difficulty: Challenging. This rating stems almost entirely from the singletrack. After the pass it gets steep and loose and is strewn with deadfall. Be careful—fully grown trees could be lying across the trail around any corner.
Trail surface: 2.7 miles on gravel road and 8.7 miles on single-track and four-wheel-drive road. The gravel road is well maintained with occasional washboards. The singletrack and four-wheel-drive tread is rugged with packed dirt; some loose, and rocky sections. Deadfall is plentiful just after Burro Pass.
Highlights: This is a true mountain experience. The *steep* downhill is a radical test of nerves and skill that requires good brakes and "hanging it out" skills. This is one to be proud of surviving. Views take in the desert and Warner and Oowah Lakes. If time and energy permit, the hiking trail from the top of Burro offers views of the region's enormity.
Land status: Manti–La Sal National Forest.
Maps: USGS Mount Tukuhniki-vatz, Mount Waas, Mount Peale, and Warner Lake.

Finding the trailhead: From Center and Main in Moab, drive 8.2 miles south on U.S. Highway 191, and turn left at the sign for the La Sal Loop Road and Ken's Lake. This road goes 0.6 mile before ending at the Loop Road (8.8 miles from town). Turn right and follow the

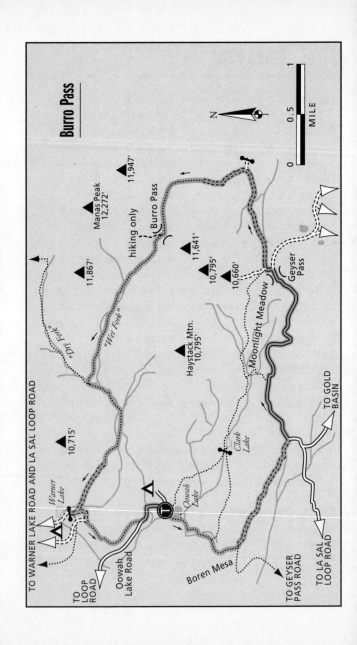

Burro Pass

N

MILE
0   0.5   1

TO WARNER LAKE ROAD AND LA SAL LOOP ROAD

10,715'

Warner Lake

"Dry Fork"

11,867'

Manas Peak
12,272'

"Wet Fork"

hiking only

Burro Pass

11,947'

TO LOOP ROAD

Oowah Lake Road

Oowah Lake

Clark Lake

Haystack Mtn.
10,795'

11,641'

10,795'

10,660'

Moonlight Meadow

Geyser Pass

Boren Mesa

TO GEYSER PASS ROAD

TO LA SAL LOOP ROAD

TO GOLD BASIN

La Sal Loop Road to mile 22.2, then turn right onto Oowah Lake Road. Take this to the top, 3.2 miles, and park at Oowah Lake.

The Ride

0.0 Go around the wooden "fence" at Oowah Lake and cross the dam. The trail peels off from the lakeshore and climbs away. All but the best trials riders will have to portage this initial climb.

0.2 The climb lessens in severity. Ride this nice singletrack, watching for the log hops at 0.3 and 0.4 mile.

0.5 Grunt past some more log jams to the top of Boren Mesa and take in the view. Follow the doubletrack as it bears left, ignoring the brown "trail" markers leading down a singletrack to Geyser Pass Road (part of Ride 13).

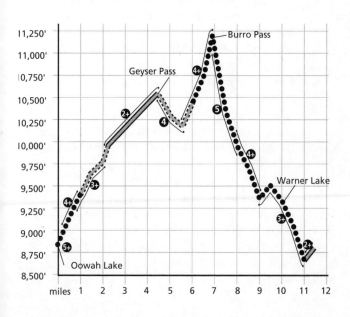

1.5   After grinding up this occasionally steep climb, pass by the singletrack spur on the left, and continue the climb on doubletrack.

2.0   Turn left on Geyser Pass Road. A brief downhill allows a chance to regain strength and get some momentum going.

2.4   Cross a cattleguard and resume climbing.

2.6   Stay on the main road as a spur to Moonlight Meadow's (Ride 13) midpoint leaves to the left.

4.5   Top of Geyser Pass! Take the left fork. Right is Ride 14, Sheepherder's Loop.

4.5   Now take the right-hand fork. Left leads to the Moonlight Meadow descent (Ride 13).

5.6   Go left on the road to Burro Pass and start the last—but worst—climb. It should be signed FR 240.

5.9   Just past the sign for Burro Pass is a gate. Cross the gate and immediately turn left. The singletrack begins about 30 feet down the fence line. Yes, the climb continues.

6.2   After a technically challenging log hop, dodge the huge fallen pine. A loose, rocky ascent awaits.

6.4   A meadow offers a brief rest from the technical harrows just endured.

6.9   Burro Pass! A humble trail sign points in two directions. To the right is a hiking path to incredible views. The bike route continues on a breakneck descent down over the lip, straight away from the sign.

7.1   Deadfall becomes a problem. *Be careful!*

8.5   The trail crosses the creek a couple of times on narrow singletrack before turning left here toward more creek crossings and Warner Lake. A sign marks the intersection.

8.9   Go straight through this intersection, passing the old road. The trail is now doubletrack and in great shape.

9.1   Registration box.

9.5   Gate.

10.0 Turn left at this gate after grabbing a peek-see at Warner Lake to the right.

10.2 Turn left on singletrack to Oowah Lake. It should be marked with a brown trail marker.

10.3 Keep left past the registration box and through a boggy section.

10.4 Cross the old road, staying straight on the singletrack as the tread gets rocky. The rocks get worse before they get better.

10.9 Turn left and climb up to Oowah Lake.

11.4 Trailhead.

13 Moonlight Meadow

Location: 23 miles east of Moab off the La Sal Loop Road.

Distance: 10.1-mile loop.

Approximate riding time: 2 hours.

Physical difficulty: Moderate. The ride starts with a gradual 4.9-mile climb, then ends with a brief series of steeps.

Technical difficulty: Moderate to challenging. The climb rates an easy to moderate, but the single-track throws in many technical tests.

Trail surface: 5 miles on gravel road; 5.1 miles on singletrack. Sections of the road may be washboarded, but it's mostly in great shape. The singletrack carves through a fertile meadow with rocks, loose dirt, roots, and boggy sections par for the course.

Highlights: This singletrack is primo stuff! It zips through aspen with barely room for the handle-bars then dives down rocky steeps for a ride that will leave finger dents in the grips. Add some log hops, ditch drops, and boggy spots with La Sal scenery and desert views for a ride that will etch its way into your personal hall of fame.

Land status: Manti–La Sal National Forest.

Maps: USGS Mount Tukuhniki-vatz, Mount Peale.

Finding the trailhead: From Center and Main in Moab, drive 8.2 miles south on U.S. Highway 191, and turn left at the sign for La Sal Loop Road and Ken's Lake. Go 0.6 mile east to the La Sal Loop Road, turn right, and drive 12 miles east and north. Turn right onto gravel Geyser Pass Road, and drive 3 miles to a pullout. Here the Trans La Sal Trail crosses Geyser Pass Road and is marked by a trail sign.

Note: The Moonlight Meadow Trail is undergoing changes to make it more environmentally friendly for mountain bikes. Portions may differ from the historic path described here, but any re-routed sections will be signed.

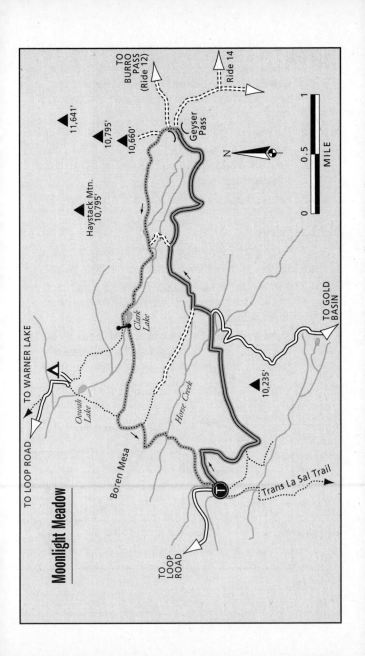

Moonlight Meadow

TO LOOP ROAD

TO WARNER LAKE

TO BURRO PASS (Ride 12)

Ride 14

11,641'

10,795'

10,660'

Geyser Pass

Haystack Mtn. 10,795'

N

MILE

0   0.5   1

Clark Lake

Oowah Lake

10,235'

TO GOLD BASIN

Boren Mesa

Horse Creek

TO LOOP ROAD

Trans La Sal Trail

The Ride

0.0 Ignore the Trans La Sal Trail for now, and head east up Geyser Pass Road. Stay on this main road until the top of the pass at mile 4.9.

1.2 The view from this sweeping turn takes in much of the desert below.

2.5 Keep left as Gold Basin Road goes right (on its own beautiful out-and-back ride).

2.7 Keep right on the main road as a spur to Boren Mesa heads left.

3.1 Cattleguard.

3.3 Keep right. This spur leads to mile 6.4 of this ride.

4.3 The view on the left foreshadows some of what's to come.

4.9 A sign marks the top of 10,600-foot Geyser Pass. Now it gets fun! Take the left fork, then immediately keep left again on doubletrack.

5.0 As the doubletrack bears right to avoid some scrubby old dead trees, bear left onto singletrack. The singletrack may be faint. Heck, it may be invisible. Have faith. If you can't find it,

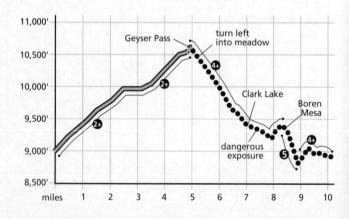

contour across the meadow. The tread becomes more apparent before it heads into the aspen groves. Whatever you do, don't stay on the doubletrack as it climbs an insanely steep hill.

5.3 The skinny ribbon of righteousness zips through the aspen. Be careful: The exit from this grove is steep and rocky.

5.7 A boggy meadow offers many cow paths and probably some cows. Be sure to stay right and down to pick up the trail proper. Try to stay dry and beware the bovine guacamole.

5.8 If you head into the pines, duck the low branch! Best to keep right and stay clear of the trees.

6.2 When the singletrack gets deep enough to become a hazard, *watch out!* A deep hole lurks ahead. The moderate-to-challenging hazard can swallow a bike and throw a rider.

6.4 A steep descent leads to the creek. Stay right and don't cross. Crossing leads up to Geyser Pass Road at mile 3.3 of this ride.

6.6 The trail has been rocky and rooty. It now crosses two creekbeds, each a technically challenging maneuver.

6.9 This pretty pond is not Clark Lake. View it from the sidehill's perilous perch and continue on.

7.2 This is Clark Lake. Options here are to drop down the switchback as described or swing through the gate for a technical descent to Oowah Lake (See Burro Pass, Ride 12).

7.3 After descending to Clark Lake, pass through the gate on the right. Follow the path to the next gate on the left, pass through it, and cross the creekbed. Pick up the trail on the other side.

7.6 Portage this exposed, eroded patch, then follow the singletrack down.

8.3 Turn left up to the top of Boren Mesa at this T junction. Right is to Oowah Lake.

8.6 Turn right and follow the trail markers. The doubletrack leads uphill to Geyser Pass Road and mile 2.7 of this ride.

8.9 The singletrack turns sharply downhill for a technically challenging descent.

9.2 Keep right at the sign for Boren Mesa.

9.4 Cross the creek, and jam it (or more likely portage) up the other side.

9.7 Take the doubletrack to the left.

10.0 Take the right here to return to the trailhead.

10.1 Back at the car, truck, van, or possibly a sport utility vehicle. A moped is right out!

14 Sheepherder's Loop

Location: 23 miles east of Moab.

Distance: 30.2-mile loop.

Approximate riding time: 4 to 7 hours.

Physical difficulty: Strenuous. This loop includes two long climbs up mountain passes and some steeps between them.

Technical difficulty: Moderate. A section through beaver ponds is hard to follow and can be technical. The Trans La Sal Trail option is wrought with challenging riding. The remainder is fairly straightforward.

Trail surface: 6 miles on gravel road; 22.7 miles on four-wheel-drive road; 1.5 miles on singletrack. The four-wheel-drive road is packed sediments with sections of rocks and ruts. The singletrack is carved into a fertile meadow overgrown with scrub oak.

Highlights: This ride circumnavigates Mount Mellenthin, Mount Peale, and Mount Tukuhnikivatz, all more than 12,000 feet, gaining expansive vistas of the surrounding country. The route is easy to follow at first, but becomes extremely faint and overgrown as it dances around beaver ponds and through a cow pasture. Count on feeling lost there, but have faith that the way will be found. The optional Trans La Sal Trail at mile 23 gives 4.2 miles of extremely technical singletrack, delivering a wide variety of rocks and roots.

Land status: Manti-La Sal National Forest.

Maps: USGS Mount Tukuhnikivatz, Mount Peale.

Finding the trailhead: From Center and Main in Moab, drive 8.2 miles south on U.S. Highway 191, and turn left at the sign for the La Sal Loop Road and Ken's Lake. This road goes 0.6 mile before ending at the Loop Road at 8.8 miles. Turn right and follow the La Sal Loop Road to mile 20.8, then turn right onto Geyser Pass Road. Head up 1.9 miles, and park where a dirt road enters from the right. If opting for the Trans La Sal portion of singletrack, use the Moonlight Meadow (Ride 13) parking area 3 miles up from the Loop Road.

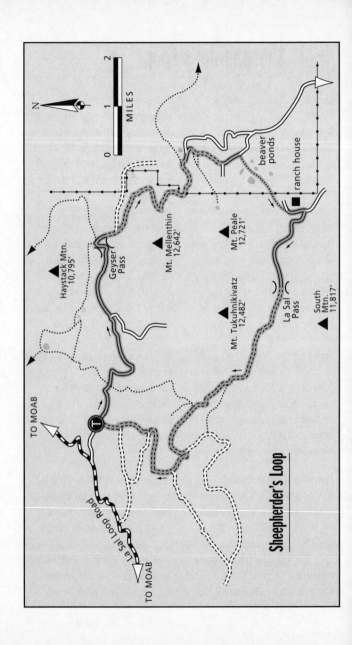

Sheepherder's Loop

Haystack Mtn.
10,795'

Geyser
Pass

Mt. Mellenthin
12,642'

Mt. Peale
12,721'

Mt. Tukuhnikivatz
12,482'

La Sal Pass

South
Mtn.
11,817'

beaver ponds

ranch house

TO MOAB

TO MOAB

La Sal Loop Road

N

MILES

0   1   2

The Ride

0.0 Begin the ascent of Geyser Pass by continuing up the gravel road, ignoring all spurs.

6.0 Geyser Pass! Stay right through an intersection and head downhill. The left fork heads to Burro Pass and Moonlight Meadow, rides 12 and 13 respectively.

6.7 The road forks; go right. Left goes to Blue Lake.

7.2 Another spur heads left and down to Blue Lake. Stay right.

9.8 Bear left through the next set of spurs, including Forest Road 723. These all explore the area between Mount Mellenthin on the right and Mount Peale on the left.

10.5 Stay right on San Juan County Road 156, and then continue to stay right past another spur. The road climbs above Dark Canyon Lake. Keep pedaling until the road turns sharply right. Take the spur to the right that leaves the road in the middle of the turn. Blue diamonds blaze the new route. Please don't use the early cutoff that climbs the embankment.

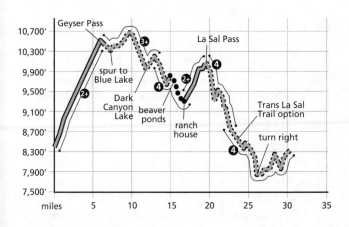

12.2 Keep left past an obscure doubletrack, and stay on this four-wheel-drive road. A nice 180-degree view opens up.

13.7 Turn left at a T intersection onto a gravel road that soon bursts into a meadow.

14.4 Turn back and to the right on a road that comes up rather suddenly after a sweeping right-hand turn. Crank up into the meadow.

14.6 Pass through a gate and immediately look for a trail marker to the left to find the overgrown roadbed.

15.0 Weave through downed trees to a wooden fence. Go through another gate, following blue diamond markers.

15.2 Continue following the blue diamonds and bear right where the trail splits at a mound of dirt. A cairn ahead should mark the next left-hand turn. If the trail hits the creek bed, turn back about 20 yards. If the navigation sounds sketchy, it is. If all else fails, contour ahead on cow trails until you run up to a fence. Follow it downhill to the gate at the 16.1-mile mark.

15.4 Pass between the closest two ponds, then run downhill. With any luck we're on the correct cow path. Pass to the right of the next pond, then to the left of the one after that, contouring at about the same elevation.

15.9 Head up into the aspens. If the trail hits a gate in 0.2 mile, go through it and continue. No gate? No sweat. Go until you run into a fence. Turn left and follow it down to the gate.

16.1 The gate. One easy-to-follow trail proceeds from the other side. Keep to the right of the log fence, and watch for bog-holes as the trail skirts to the right of a ranch house.

16.5 Turn right onto the ranch's access road.

16.9 Keep right, then turn right onto a gravel road.

18.3 Keep left past the spur to Beaver Lake.

19.1 Pass Forest Road 238 as it heads left to Medicine Lake.

19.4 La Sal Pass. Stay right after enjoying the view. Forest Road 237 goes left and is worth exploring, but our route continues straight down the road, which quickly becomes wrought with rocks.

20.2 Pass a pond and continue downhill.

21.2 A road joins from the left.

21.3 Go right on Forest Road 700. At the bottom of this descent, a hairpin turn goes left just before a large rock field. Keep your momentum if you want to clean the rocks (a technically challenging maneuver).

22.3 FR 700 contours straight ahead. Instead, turn left onto Forest Road 701 down the switchback since FR 700's midsection is absent.

22.5 Keep right as a road enters from the left.

23.0 Shortly after FR 700 rejoins on the right, a rough trail heads up the steep meadow on the right. This is the Trans La Sal Trail, which leads back to Geyser Pass Road via 4.2 miles of extremely technical trail. An old claim stake marks the meadow. Let's bypass the obstacle course—stay on the main road heading downhill.

24.2 After crossing a few streams, the road forks. Take the right route up and over the ridge. Left continues down 4 miles to Pack Creek about 1.5 miles from the La Sal Loop Road and an 11-mile uphill ride back to the car.

25.9 Drop down an extremely loose and steep section and turn right where the road forks. Don't miss this right-hand turn. The left fork runs onto the Pack Creek Ranch, requiring a long climb back to the car.

27.5 The route passes a spring and contours around the lower limb of Mount Tukuhnikivatz then drops into Dorry Canyon.

27.7 Turn right and head uphill. Left runs down another fun four-wheel-drive path, ending up on the La Sal Loop Road and leaving a 2-mile uphill ride to Geyser Pass Road.

29.2 Stay right passing yet another spur to the Loop Road. It connects with the previous spur.

30.2 Geyser Pass Road and the trailhead.

Trans La Sal Option: This rugged singletrack requires a bit of info to keep you on track. About 1.2 miles from the initial turn, pass through a gate and descend into a meadow and cross to the cabin. Behind and to the left of the cabin lies a portage that scrambles up to the trail. It is also possible to reach the same place by following the four-wheel-drive road downhill and out of the meadow, then turning right at the cairn about 0.2 mile ahead. This second option is easy to miss, but lost souls may stumble onto a great view into Dorry Canyon.

15 Porcupine Rim

Location: 10 miles east of Moab.

Distance: 15-mile one-way with a shuttle or 31.2-mile loop.

Approximate riding time: 2 to 4 hours. The loop takes 4 to 7 hours.

Physical difficulty: Moderately strenuous. The first climb is fairly extended, but after 4 miles it's all downhill. As a loop, this is definitely strenuous and often dusty.

Technical difficulty: Challenging. The majority of the ride is solid moderate-to-challenging work up and down ledges on steep, rocky slopes. The singletrack is famous for riding that challenges even elite riders. Cocky riders often take soil samples home along with a serving of crow pie.

Trail surface: 11.7 miles on four-wheel-drive road; 3.3 miles on singletrack. The four-wheel-drive road is full of bedrock steps laid down on packed dirt with occasional sandy spots. The singletrack is packed dirt when it's not climbing, dodging, and hopping the encroaching boulders.

Highlights: Next to the Slickrock Trail (Ride 1), this is perhaps the most notorious of Moab's rides. The view from the rim is as breathtaking as the cigarettes whose ads use the same background. It's definitely an E-ticket ride to Moab's supreme singletrack. The singletrack has received mixed reviews; some find it too technical for their taste, but it induces perma-grin to those who like boulder boppin' and ledge droppin' along vertigo-inducing cliffsides. When ridden as a loop, it includes the climb up Sand Flats Road, which can get extremely busy and dusty during the high season, and it returns along narrow Utah Highway 128. For shuttle information see Appendix F.

Land status: BLM.

Maps: USGS Rill Creek, Moab, Windows.

Finding the trailhead: From Center Street and Main in Moab, go 0.3 mile east on Center. Turn right onto 400 West and go 0.4 mile,

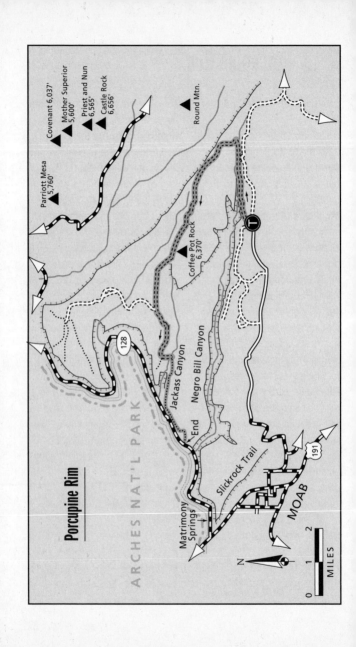

Porcupine Rim

Parriott Mesa 5,760'

Covenant 6,037'
Mother Superior 5,600'
Priest and Nun 6,565'
Castle Rock 6,656'

Round Mtn.

Coffee Pot Rock 6,370'

ARCHES NAT'L PARK

128

Jackass Canyon

End

Negro Bill Canyon

Slickrock Trail

Matrimony Springs

191

MOAB

N

0   1   2
MILES

then left onto Mill Creek at Dave's Corner Market. Go 0.5 mile on Mill Creek to a stop sign and continue straight onto Sand Flats Road. (Look for a cemetery on the left as a landmark.) Stay on Sand Flats and pay the appropriate fee at the gate (bike: $2.00; car: $5.00; camp: $8.00). Continue on this road 7 miles to an information kiosk and three big stock tanks sitting by the road. This is the trailhead. The road is dirt from mile 4.0 onward and gets washboarded, but it is drivable in a passenger car. The trailhead has a pit toilet. There is no running water, and parking is limited, so leave room for others. Overflow parking is available 0.1 mile back toward town. An alternate trailhead requiring a high-clearance vehicle is 2 miles farther up the road.

The Ride

0.0   From the trailhead registration box, head down the trail, left from Sand Flats Road.

0.2   Stay right. The spur to the left heads along the rim of Negro Bill Canyon and connects to Sand Flats Road 2 miles west of this ride's trailhead.

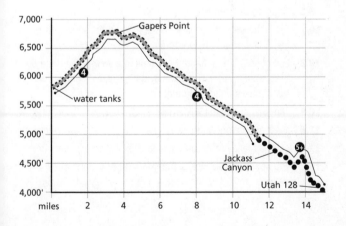

1.5 Stay right and up as a spur peels off to the left.

1.6 Stay on the main road. The road joining from the right is from the high-clearance portion of Sand Flats Road.

2.4 This transition is pretty tricky as the route dips into the ditch then, presto-chango, it climbs out.

3.1 Look off to the right for the first views of Castle Valley.

3.8 Climb to another viewpoint.

3.9 Some techy steps lead to Gapers Point. The road continues on playing tag with the rim for a bit. See the map for the names of all the famous rocks of cigarette-ad country.

4.9 A welcome smooth stretch for 0.2 mile.

5.2 Go straight through this signed four-way intersection.

5.4 Stay right at all the forks from here through mile 7.6. Arrows should point the way.

7.8 Keep left at this signed fork.

8.0 A surprise move out of the sand. Another sand trap lurks ahead.

8.2 The trail heads left at this fork.

8.5 Straight on through the four-way intersection.

9.1 Once again, keep left.

10.7 Cross the slickrock to pick up the road on the same heading. Cairns should help with navigation.

10.8 Left here. The right-hand fork heads to a view of Big Bend on the Colorado River. The trail may be blocked off with sticks, but it makes a nice side trip.

10.9 The road enters the Wilderness Study Area.

11.6 Right at this fork where two signs were placed. How special.

11.7 Let's get ready to rrrrummmmble! The singletrack starts here.

12.2 The ride is now in Jackass Canyon, with Utah 128 visible below.

12.6 Vertigo-inducing section. To paraphrase famous useless advice, "Just don't look down." Here comes trouble.

14.4 The trail heads left around a boulder, then down and across the gulch. Definitely technically challenging. Things ease up from here.

14.9 This last hill is a wee bit sandy.

15.0 Welcome to Utah 128. Where did you park your shuttle car? Turn left to head back to town if doing a loop. An underpass in Lion's Park aids in crossing U.S. Highway 191.

16 Flat Pass

Location: 10 miles south of Moab near Ken's Lake.

Distance: 17.4-mile loop.

Approximate riding time: 2 to 4 hours.

Physical difficulty: Moderately strenuous. The initial climbs are strenuous, but they allow for recovery. Obstacles may make this trail seem aerobically tougher.

Technical difficulty: Moderate to challenging. Paved and gravel roads offer no significant technical challenges, but the four-wheel-drive portion rates a solid moderate to challenging, with challenging patches demanding constant attention.

Trail surface: 9.1 miles on four-wheel-drive road; 1.5 miles on gravel road; 6.8 miles on paved road. The four-wheel-drive road offers lots of slickrock and bedrock ledges. Sand becomes a problem after crossing Mill Creek.

Highlights: Flat Pass delivers a lot of what the region offers. Petroglyphs and pioneers' inscriptions show the area's popularity through the ages. Views into Canyonlands National Park are nothing short of spectacular, and the immediate surroundings include a canyon with huge, vertical rock walls split in two by a perennial creek lined with greenery. The four-wheel-drive portion starts with ledgy technical tests and finishes with cobblestone and sandy creek crossings. Nothing stirs emotions like a mile of deep sand. Yum.

Land status: BLM land surrounded by private holdings and a travel-restricted region.

Maps: USGS Kane Springs, Rill Creek.

Finding the trailhead: From Center Street in Moab, drive 8.2 miles south on U.S. Highway 191 and turn left at the sign for the La Sal Loop Road and Ken's Lake. This road goes 0.6 mile before ending at the Loop Road (8.8 miles from town). Turn right and follow the Loop Road 1.5 miles as it bends left past a gravel pit. Turn left onto the paved Ken's Lake access road, then go 0.6 mile and turn left into the parking area.

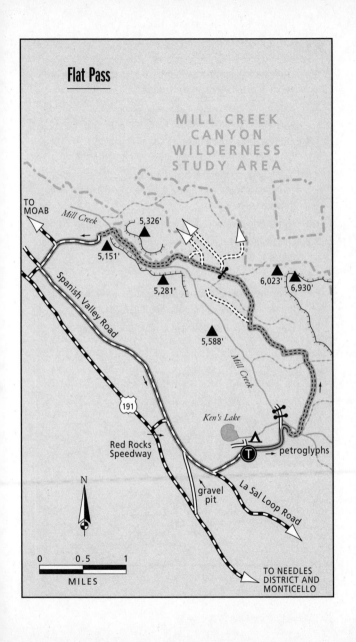

Flat Pass

MILL CREEK
CANYON
WILDERNESS
STUDY AREA

TO MOAB

Mill Creek

5,326'

5,151'

5,281'

6,023' 6,930'

Spanish Valley Road

5,588'

Mill Creek

191

Ken's Lake

Red Rocks Speedway

T

petroglyphs

N

gravel pit

La Sal Loop Road

0   0.5   1
MILES

TO NEEDLES
DISTRICT AND
MONTICELLO

The Ride

0.0 From the parking area on Ken's Lake Road, turn left and pedal east on the main gravel road.

1.3 Stay on the main road. A side road going left offers a close look at a man-made waterfall and some petroglyphs.

1.5 After crossing the cattleguard and descending, turn right at a T intersection (the road left enters private property).

1.8 Inscriptions on the rock here deserve a look and mark a "don't-miss" left-hand turn. Cross the creek, and follow the road up to the right.

1.9 This slickrock zone can be confusing. Follow the tire marks.

2.1 This technically moderate-to-challenging ascent is a sign of things to come.

2.6 Watch the drop into the wash.

3.3 Enjoy the view west, then follow the trail arrow that points the way. Avoid the old roadbed on the right.

3.6 Stay left where the road splits. Climb out of the wash on

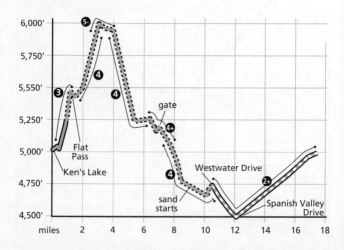

slickrock. A series of technically challenging maneuvers awaits as the route switchbacks right. The next mile remains fairly technical.

5.4 Stay right at this fork.

5.5 Another fork; stay left.

5.6 Go straight through this intersection. An arrow points the way if it has survived the region's world-class sign hunters.

5.8 A nice luge run is interrupted by this sandy turn.

5.9 Climb on slickrock to a left-hand turn at a T intersection.

6.9 A long downhill ends with a technically moderate-to-challenging ascent.

7.0 Pass through the gate, and take a left at the next fork.

7.4 Keep on the left side of this slickrock. Look for a rock cairn marking the road.

8.1 Turn left and down, then keep left at this confusing intersection. A technically moderate-to-challenging descent awaits.

8.5 Keep right. The road is riddled with cobblestones and enters the canyon floor.

9.2 Cross Mill Creek. Here comes the sand.

9.7 Cross the creek. Yup, it's still sandy.

9.8 A brief respite from the sand and another creek crossing.

10.2 Solid ground at last. Follow the switchback up and to the left. Anything else is trespassing.

10.3 Climb a steep pitch, past a gate and onto sandy tread again.

10.6 Turn left onto paved Westwater Drive.

11.7 Turn left onto Canyonlands Circle. Stop at the stop sign, then continue through the intersection.

12.1 Turn left onto Spanish Valley Drive.

13.9 Bear left to remain on Spanish Valley Drive.

15.3 La Sal Loop Road enters from the right. Stay straight.

16.8 Turn left toward Ken's Lake on the paved access road.

17.4 Loop complete. Go find the car.

17 Prostitute Behind the Rocks— Prostitute's Behind—or A Nice Butte

Location: 13 miles south of Moab.

Distance: 20.3-mile lariat-shaped loop.

Approximate riding time: 1.5 to 3 hours.

Physical difficulty: Moderately easy. The initial ups and downs are long and gradual; later hills are shorter and steeper. The final thrust to Prostitute Butte is a definite grind. But after that climax it's a gentle push to a wild downhill release. Without recent rain the sand makes the ride aerobically tougher. If length isn't important, heading straight for the Prostitute at mile 4.5 cuts 8.2 miles off the ride.

Technical difficulty: Moderate. Expect mostly smooth sailing with some small ledges, slickrock, and sand in washes and around the butte.

Trail surface: 4 miles on gravel road; 16.3 miles on four-wheel-drive trails. The trail is mostly

hard with intermittent soft, sandy sections. From the butte onward the track erodes into slick grooves and bare rock, then returns to gentle tread for the leg home. Rain mixed with bovine activity can make the gravel road quite rough.

Highlights: Prostitute Butte boasts two arches, and the technical jaunt out to Hunters Canyon Rim offers a bird's-eye view of the lonely canyon. The ride then is a bump-and-grind downhill back to the main road. To make this much easier, go straight for Prostitute Butte at mile 4.5. Options exist for the whole family here. For those who like it hard and fast, connect with Ride 18. The main road runs all the way to Pritchett Arch (Ride 24) for a nice, long shuttle ride.

Land status: BLM.

Maps: USGS Kane Springs, Trough Springs.

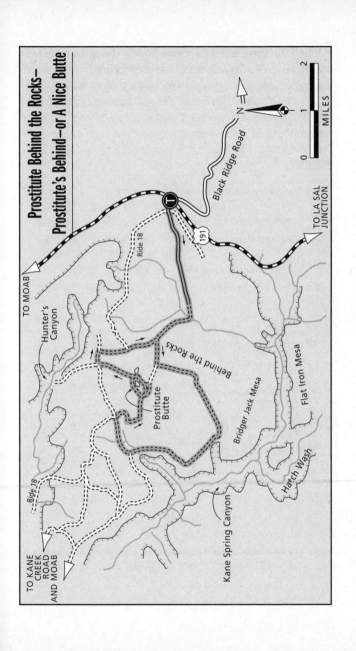

Prostitute Behind the Rocks—
Prostitute's Behind—or A Nice Butte

TO MOAB

Hunter's Canyon

Ride 18

Ride 18

TO KANE CREEK ROAD AND MOAB

Behind the Rocks

Prostitute Butte

Kane Spring Canyon

Bridger Jack Mesa

Hatch Wash

Flat Iron Mesa

Black Ridge Road

191

TO LA SAL JUNCTION

N

0   1   2
MILES

Finding the trailhead: From Center Street in Moab, drive 13.1 miles south on U.S. Highway 191. Turn right onto a dirt road that appears just after the highway climbs a hill and shortly after mile marker 113. Cross the cattleguard and find a place to park. High-clearance vehicles can continue to the alternative trailhead 2.3 miles down the route to shave off the final climb.

The Ride

0.0   Leave the parking area on the main dirt road. Head north in the direction of Moab, with US 191 to the right. Many faint spurs split off in all directions, but the main road is obvious.

0.4   The road forks; stay left. To go Behind the Rocks turn right—it's no fun riding clockwise. The 24 Hours of Moab Race loops counterclockwise for its course.

2.3   Keep right, on the main road. This is the alternate trailhead.

2.6   Keep left, on the main road.

2.9   Keep right and cross the soft, sandy wash.

3.0   Follow the sign toward Pritchett Arch and go right.

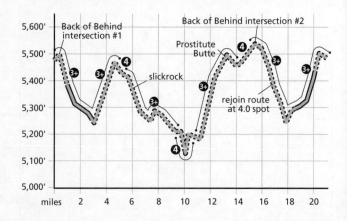

3.2 Stay on the main road as right-hand spurs go to the sand dunes.

3.6 The sand and rock grab the tires here.

3.7 *Sand trap! Aooga! Sand trap!*

4.0 Keep left. The road right is used on the return trip (mile 16.3).

4.5 As the hill tapers off, a doubletrack leaves to the left. Follow the doubletrack toward Kane Springs Canyon. Remaining on the main road leads straight to Prostitute Butte and rejoins the route below at mile 12.7.

5.6 A spur to the right heads down the slickrock. Take this to hook up with the doubletrack that heads through the small valley. A sand trap mars the start. Do *not* take the very faint doubletrack to the right (if you even see it).

7.2 The road forks. The left-hand track is more worn, but it's the nearly indiscernible right-hand track you want. Be looking for it and follow it with the canyon on the left.

7.8 Stay right at this sandy fork.

8.7 A cairn marks the right-hand turn at this fork. The canyon views get better and better. The tread now has some slick-rock candy and packed dirt.

8.9 A technically moderate-to-challenging rock step.

9.5 Another moderate-to-challenging rock step.

10.2 Crank through the sand and slickrock in this wash and up the other side. The head of the canyon is quite a sight.

10.4 Right back onto the main road. Ignore any spurs.

11.3 Anticipation builds as Prostitute Butte looms up to the right, and you grunt through another sand trap.

11.5 Three-way intersection. Turn right and head up to the butte.

12.7 Turn left, then follow the road all the way around the rock to see the naked beauty of both arches. On the next time around, keep straight as you cross the saddle and join the doubletrack to the north.

14.2 Four-way intersection. Turn right. Straight goes to Hunter's Canyon and is definitely worth the technical and physical effort. Left heads down to the 11.3-mile point.

14.5 Keep right on the red road. Watch the ruts, then unclamp those brakes as the road races to meet itself at mile 4.0.

15.5 Stay straight on the main road. Left here runs to the Behind the Rocks Trail (Ride 18), but in the wrong direction.

16.3 The 4-mile point. Turn left to retrace the route back to the trailhead. Ahh . . . was it good for you?

18 Behind the Rocks Trail

Location: 13 miles south of Moab.

Distance: 19.3-mile one-way. 28-mile loop (see map).

Approximate riding time: 3 hours plus shuttle; 6 hours as a loop.

Physical difficulty: Moderate. The initial climb strikes without a warm-up and is followed by a series of steeps in quick succession. Despite this heart-pounding start, the overall route is downhill.

Technical difficulty: Challenging. The first portion of trail borders on insanity. A huge hill of sand is a challenge to ride downhill, and many of the washes feature chest-high drops. If you survive that, the ride mellows slightly, still delivering ledges, ruts, rocks, and sand—what true phat heads call phun.

Trail surface: 19.3 miles on four-wheel-drive road. This is a brutal trail with deep sand, ledges up to 4 feet high, and the gamut of common obstacles.

Highlights: This is a mentally tiring ride demanding constant concentration. The route initially follows a portion of the 24 Hours of Moab bike race course, which is so technical you may wonder what made you pick this trail. A fun ride for those ready for a wide variety of challenges. It also loops well by turning left at mile 13.2 to return via a technically mellow road to Prostitute Butte (see map for options). The sand hill at mile 2.1 can be avoided by using roads from Ride 17 and rejoining this route at mile 4.9.

Land status: BLM and about 100 yards of private property with a required $1.00 bike toll (see Ride 28 for a no-cost option).

Maps: USGS Kane Springs Canyon, Trough Springs, and Moab.

Finding the trailhead: To do this ride as a point-to-point trip, leave a shuttle vehicle at the Kane Creek Boulevard Trailhead. From

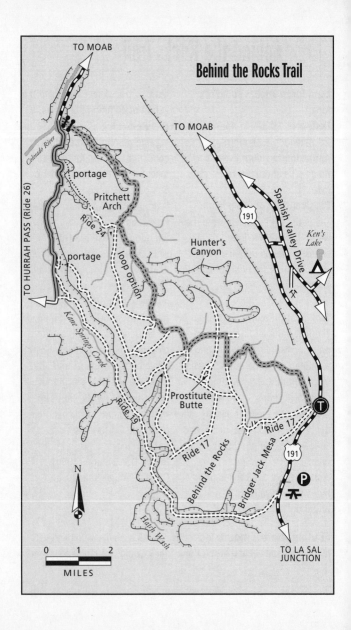

Behind the Rocks Trail

TO MOAB

TO MOAB

Colorado River

portage

Pritchett Arch

Ride 24

portage

TO HURRAH PASS (Ride 26)

loop option

Kane Springs Creek

Ride 19

Hunter's Canyon

Spanish Valley Drive

191

Ken's Lake

Prostitute Butte

Ride 17

Behind the Rocks

Bridger Jack Mesa

Ride 17

T

191

P

Hatch Wash

N

TO LA SAL JUNCTION

0   1   2
MILES

Center Street in Moab, drive 0.7 mile south on U.S. Highway 191 to
Kane Creek Boulevard, and turn right. The turn is between the Star
Diner and McDonald's. At 1.5 miles stay left through a "Dangerous
Intersection" on Kane Creek Boulevard (it appears to be a left turn).
About 5.5 miles from Center Street, look for the trailhead on the left.
Additional parking is just up the road. Leave the shuttle vehicle here
and retrace the route back to US 191. Turn right and drive 12.4 miles
south on US 191. Just after climbing a hill and passing mile marker
113, turn right onto a dirt road. Park here. This same trailhead is
used for Ride 17.

The Ride

0.0 From the parking area pedal west down the main road. Many
faint spurs split off right and left, but the main road is obvious.

0.4 The road forks; go right. (Left is the route for Ride 17, Prostitute Behind the Rocks.)

1.3 Stay on the main road. A hard-to-see spur goes right and
down to US 191.

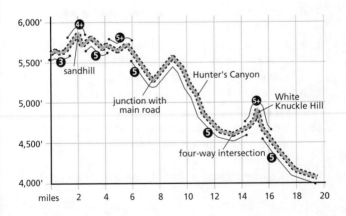

1.7 Turn left following the main road. The track becomes sandy and eroded as it runs along the edge of a wilderness study area. A spur road on the right heads into the study area and is off-limits to bikes.

2.1 This huge sandhill downhill is the reason to pedal this ride east to west.

2.5 A dangerous wash-drop lies ahead! With but one gentle stretch, the next 2 miles are very technical.

4.9 Turn right. This brief section is shared with Ride 17.

6.3 A crossroads; go straight. Another steep reason to ride from east to west lies ahead.

7.3 Turn right onto the main road to Pritchett Arch, then immediately turn right off of the road. The route heads uphill, then edges along the rugged hillside.

8.6 Turn right here. Missing this turn leads to the road used in the loop option mentioned at mile 13.2.

9.9 After dropping down this near-cliff pitch, turn right. The roads to the left head back to the main, less technical road used in the return loop. Simply stay on the easily navigated main road, avoiding any spurs.

11.0 Drop over several bedrock ledges, and enjoy the technical run in Hunter's Canyon.

13.2 At a well-used intersection, turn right toward Pritchett Arch (Ride 24). Straight goes to Gatherer's Canyon, and left heads back to Prostitute Butte for a nice, long loop.

15.0 Top of White Knuckle Hill. Hang on for a totally gnarly descent, dude.

15.3 The road forks. Go right to stay on the main route. Go left if you want to visit Pritchett Arch (a connector road rejoins the route at mile 15.5).

15.6 Drop down yet another extremely steep hill and turn left.

16.8 Keep left here as a spur climbs to the right.

17.6 Cross the wash.

18.6 Keep rolling through basketball-size cobblestones (aka babyheads), and hop a couple of ledges.

19.2 Toll gate. Cross the gate and pay the $1.00 toll at the next gate. Now go find your shuttle vehicle.

19.3 Kane Creek Boulevard Trailhead.

19 Kane Springs Canyon

Location: 15.5 miles south of Moab.

Distance: 20.2-mile one-way. Don't even think of doing this as an out-and-back! A long, clockwise loop is possible with the Prostitute and Behind the Rocks routes (see Rides 17 and 18).

Approximate riding time: 3 to 5 hours, depending upon creek and sand conditions. Start early if considering the daylong loop, and have a backup plan that includes extra food and extra chain.

Physical difficulty: Moderate. The sand can be exhausting, but the ride runs gradually downhill.

Technical difficulty: Challenging. The cobblestone tread, creek crossings, and sand all demand concentration to maintain the necessary momentum.

Trail surface: 6.7 miles on gravel road; 13.5 miles on four-wheel-drive road. For 9.5 miles the four-wheel-drive road crosses and travels in Kane Springs Creek on cobblestone and sand before becoming hard-packed with some eroded ruts. The gravel road is well maintained.

Highlights: This is a wet one. Kane Creek usually has an ample flow, and the ride dives right in to it. The sand is rideable for the most part, but it gums up drivetrains! The canyon induces claustrophobia with towering, crumbling walls. It's almost a relief when Hurrah Pass comes into view. As a loop with the Pritchett Arch ride and the numerous roads Behind the Rocks, this ride is extremely exhausting. Take along a good set of tools and nourishment—it's a long way back to civilization and the sand is tough on equipment. Did you pack a chain tool?

Land status: BLM.

Maps: USGS Kane Springs, Trough Springs.

Finding the trailhead: From Center Street in Moab, drive 15.4 miles south on U.S. Highway 191. A roadside rest area is directly across from the trailhead. Parking is available at the trailhead and

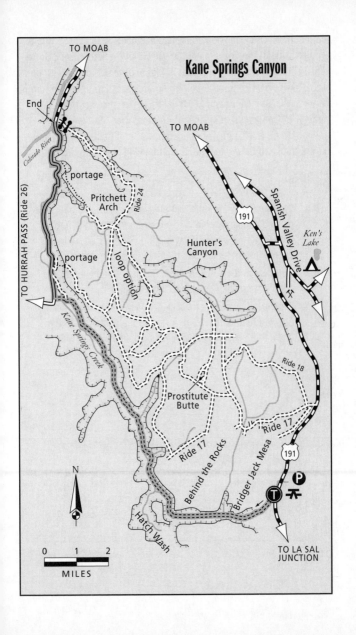

Kane Springs Canyon

TO MOAB

End

Colorado River

portage

Pritchett Arch

Ride 24

TO HURRAH PASS (Ride 26)

portage

loop option

Kane Springs Creek

TO MOAB

191

Spanish Valley Drive

Ken's Lake

Hunter's Canyon

Ride 18

Prostitute Butte

Ride 17

Behind the Rocks

Ride 17

Bridger Jack Mesa

191

P

T

Hatch Wash

N

0   1   2
MILES

TO LA SAL JUNCTION

the rest area. Obey any posted parking restrictions. To do this ride as a point-to-point trip, leave a shuttle vehicle at the Kane Creek Boulevard Trailhead. From Center Street in Moab, drive 0.7 mile south on U.S. Highway 191 to Kane Creek Boulevard, and turn right. The turn is between the Star Diner and McDonald's. At 1.5 miles stay left through a "Dangerous Intersection" on Kane Creek Boulevard (it appears to be a left turn). About 5.5 miles from Center Street, look for the trailhead on the left. Additional parking is just up the road.

The Ride

0.0 Directly across from the rest area, a road leaves the highway, passes through a whip gate, crosses a cattleguard, and drops into the wash. Follow it down. Stay left, avoiding the asphalt road that crosses the wash and climbs.

0.1 Turn right and follow the wash. The ride goes right into the cobblestone-filled creek bed. Time to get dirty.

2.3 The creek has some tiny, slickrock falls at this confluence. Stay left here on the road. A spur to the right crosses the creek to a section of singletrack complete with an old

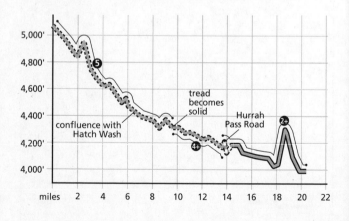

bridge. It is rideable, but you will have to portage back to the road to continue.

2.8 The road rises above the canyon floor. The old bridge is visible below. For the next 7 miles, riders must blast through the creek crossings and the sand between them.

6.3 Hatch Wash enters from the left as the route completes a mile-long bend to the right.

9.5 The tread leaves the sand for higher, harder ground. It might be a good idea to degunk your drivetrain here.

13.5 Turn right onto the gravel road (Kane Creek Boulevard, aka Hurrah Pass Road), and follow it to the shuttle vehicle.

20.2 Kane Creek main parking area. It's 5 miles to Moab from here.

20 Flat Iron Mesa

Location: 19 miles south of Moab.

Distance: 13-mile out-and-back.

Approximate riding time: 1 hour with half a day's worth of possibilities.

Physical difficulty: Easy. For Moab, this is an easy ride, though a couple of the hills may push the standard definition given in this book. Depending on how many side routes you explore, the rating can rise all the way to strenuous.

Technical difficulty: Easy to moderate. The main obstacles are the small erosion ruts that often surprise riders who ignore them. The side routes are awarded moderate-to-challenging status.

Trail surface: 13 miles on gravel road. The road gets rough and eroded in spots, but it's mostly smooth rolling on packed dirt.

The side routes tend to be extremely eroded and broken. As usual, sand is never scarce.

Highlights: This scenic, gentle ride offers lots of tricky terrain on the side, making it great as a family ride. Even hybrid bikes do well on the main route, while those seeking more challenge can check out the spur roads. An optional route in Kane Springs Canyon heads down a side road to what I call Surround-Sound Point, where echoes even come from behind! Another fun, more technical option is to ride along Hatch Canyon. A group of riders of various abilities could meet at the end point, take in the expansive depths of the Kane and Hatch Canyons' confluence, and explore back to the car. Nice.

Land status: BLM.

Maps: USGS La Sal Junction, Eightmile Rock.

Finding the trailhead: From Center and Main in Moab, drive 20.8 miles south on U.S. Highway 191. Shortly after passing an industrial site full of pipes, look for a road going right. It is up the hill from the plant and should be signed. Turn right and park. Be sure to leave room for vehicles to pass.

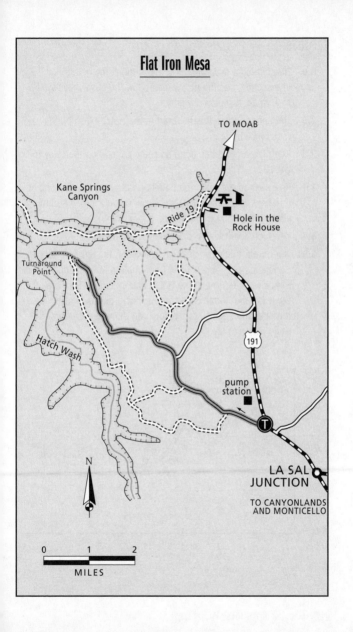

Flat Iron Mesa

Kane Springs Canyon

Ride 19

TO MOAB

Hole in the
Rock House

Turnaround
Point

Hatch Wash

US 191

pump
station

T

N

LA SAL
JUNCTION

TO CANYONLANDS
AND MONTICELLO

0   1   2
MILES

The Ride

0.0 Head straight down the road and through the immediate intersection, bearing northwest. Follow the easily navigated main road, avoiding any spurs.

2.0 The spur on the left is the start of the Hatch Wash option (see below).

2.5 Keep left around this bend as spurs go right on their way to US 191.

3.4 Keep left on the main road. Right heads down to a low point that links into Kane Springs Canyon. Or once did. It stops short of the canyon and leaves a long climb back.

5.4 Keep left. Right leads to Surround-Sound Point.

6.5 The payoff. That's Hatch Wash Canyon on the left and Kane Springs Canyon on the right. Contemplate the optional routes while returning. The Hatch option joins at the 5-mile point (at about mile 8 on the way back) and is hard to see. It makes more sense to try Hatch on the way out and Kane while coming back.

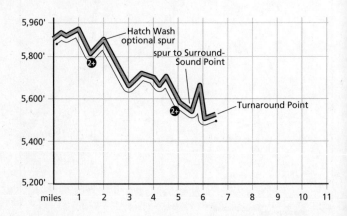

Hatch Wash Option: Start the ride as described above, but turn left onto the spur at mile 2 and continue toward the canyon's rim. Stay right where another spur joins in. Following this route hinges on finding a right turn that occurs just before an old drilling pad. But continue past this turn to the sandstone blob dead ahead for the view. Back at the crucial turn (now a left), follow the new road along the rim. Another sandstone blob marks the right-hand turn back to the main route at mile 5.

Kane Springs Canyon Option: At the 5.4-mile mark, head north (right on the way out, left coming back), and follow the road as it drops toward the rim. This track gets progressively more difficult. With the rim in sight, an obscure left allows a bit more access. Stop on the slickrock and hike to the rim. See if you can find Surround-Sound Point.

21 Boxcar Bridge

Location: 50 miles south of Moab in the Canyon Rims Recreational Area.

Distance: 21.4-mile loop.

Approximate riding time: 2.5 to 4 hours.

Physical difficulty: Moderately strenuous. Most of the ride has a gradual grade, but a couple of climbs are strenuous (and sandy, too).

Technical difficulty: Moderate. Some eroded sections are moderate to challenging, but the majority of the ride is on mild, rustic road.

Trail surface: 7.3 miles on gravel; 14.1 miles on four-wheel-drive roads. The four-wheel-drive roads begin as packed dirt, then become sandy and eroded in the canyon.

Highlights: Beginning with a gradual spin, the ride turns technical as it dives into the isolated head of Trout Water Canyon. Boxcar Bridge comes into view high on a hill, then the trail turns into a cottonwood-lined wash near an old homestead. Sand traps force most riders to push in a couple of spots, but such desert solitude is worth it. Other people are rarely seen on this route.

Land status: Canyon Rims Recreational District.

Map: USGS Eightmile Rock.

Finding the trailhead: From Center and Main in Moab, drive 34.2 miles south on U.S. Highway 191 to the Canyon Rims Recreational Area. Turn right on County Road 133, also known as the Needles Overlook Road. Follow this paved road 15.1 miles west to a Y junction. Take the right-hand fork (Anticline Road), and drive 0.7 mile north. Turn right onto Eightmile Rock Road (County Road 132) and park.

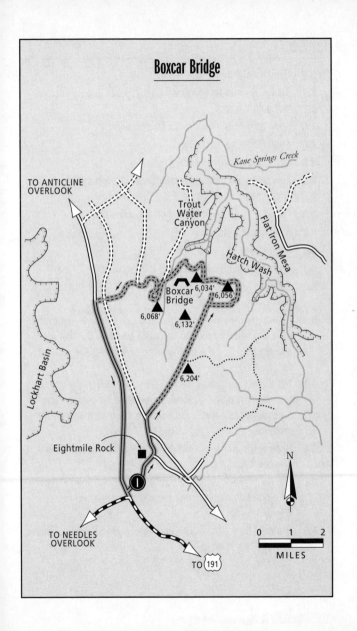

Boxcar Bridge

Kane Springs Creek

TO ANTICLINE
OVERLOOK

Trout
Water
Canyon

Hatch Wash

Flat Iron Mesa

Lockhart Basin

Boxcar
Bridge

6,034'

6,056'

6,068'

6,132'

6,204'

Eightmile Rock

TO NEEDLES
OVERLOOK

TO 191

N

0   1   2
MILES

The Ride

0.0 Head up Eightmile Rock Road.

1.1 Briefly descend to a fork and go left, past the old structures built into the rock.

1.6 Keep right here, heeding the Danger sign.

2.0 Bear left onto a gravel road.

2.2 Cross a bright yellow cattleguard.

2.3 Turn right onto an arrow-straight road through the brush. The ride remains on this main road for a few miles.

3.9 Pass by the cattle trough, ignoring spur roads.

4.2 A spur goes right; keep left.

4.4 A spur goes left; keep right.

4.7 Crest a small rise. Junipers dot the landscape.

5.2 The road forks; go left. The road becomes rougher and increasingly overgrown.

5.9 A faint road—more like overgrown doubletrack—leaves to the right and you'll follow it to complete the loop. But first go straight for 0.25 mile to a viewpoint well worth the extra distance.

6.15 Top the hill and roll to the viewpoint. Trout Water Canyon lies ahead, with rippled slickrock below, while the ever-present La Sals frame the horizon. Backtrack to the road mentioned at mile 5.9.

6.4 Back at the 5.9 spot. Take the fork less traveled, which is now a left turn.

6.7 The doubletrack becomes patchy rock, gravel, and sand on an eroded descent through rock outcroppings and old-growth junipers.

7.3 The road turns left up a sandy hill followed by a soft, sandy descent. This is a fun surf!

8.4 The tread is heavily eroded after this turn. Watch the ruts! Cross a sandy wash, and claw up a brutally sandy hill. Ride the erosion ruts for any chance of reaching the top without pushing. Ignore the numerous cow paths braiding off the main track.

8.9 Top the hill only to tackle another, more rideable hill. The upcoming descent is gradual on a sand and grass double-track.

9.3 The road bears left. Don't be fooled by the cow paths.

9.7 Hang on for a rough and rutted descent, with some smooth spots tossed in for good measure. Wheee!

10.1 Bounce through a sand and slickrock wash, then scramble up a loose, rock-strewn climb.

10.4 Look north for the view over Trout Water Canyon to Prostitute Butte and the Behind the Rocks region.

10.9 Boxcar Bridge can easily be seen high up on the butte ahead and to the left.

11.4 Cross another wash.

11.8 Ugh . . . another loose, eroded, rocky climb. Rate it at moderate to challenging.

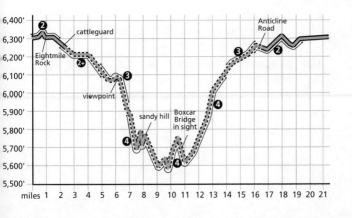

12.2 Keep right on the doubletrack as a cow trail heads left.

12.4 Grab the brakes for an eroded descent with a technically challenging spot at mile 12.5.

12.6 T into a sandy doubletrack and turn left. Cross the wash. Right is the return portion of the Trout Water Canyon Trail (see Appendix A: Additional Rides).

12.9 The road is still sandy as it goes into a wash. Follow the wash to the left for 100 yards, and then exit on the right-hand side.

13.2 Into the wash again, then out the left side toward the huge cottonwoods. Pass through the gate in the grove.

13.4 Wobble up the gullied road to a switchback fork. Stay right and up. Left leads to Trout Water Spring. The road becomes less sandy, but small sand traps (baby bunkers?) still lurk.

14.2 A not-so-neonatal sand trap.

14.4 Bear right on the slickrock to pick up the trail.

14.6 Grunt up a soft climb.

14.9 Top. Stay left as a road joins from the right (the final leg of the Trout Water Canyon loop).

15.4 The tread improves. Keep right at a Y junction, and stay on the main road from here to Anticline Road.

16.3 Anticline Road. Stop to enjoy the view through Lockhart Canyon and beyond. Then look for traffic and turn left, pedaling south on rolling gravel road.

21.4 Loop complete. Where's a tall glass of lemonade when you need one?

22 Colorado River Overlook

Location: 70 miles south of Moab in Canyonlands National Park.

Distance: 14.6 miles out-and-back.

Approximate riding time: 2 to 3 hours.

Physical difficulty: Moderate. The road grade is pretty gradual; the main energy drains come in small doses. Save some water for the final 2.5-mile climb on the return trip.

Technical difficulty: Moderate. This makes a good first ride in the Needles District to gauge skills. Hazards—mainly eroded ruts and potholes—are well exposed.

Trail surface: 14.6 miles on four-wheel-drive road. The road is mainly packed dirt with some exposed rock and occasional eroded patches.

Highlights: Gazing down on the Colorado River after pumping through the desert puts things into perspective—life is good. This is a great way to experience this section of Canyonlands without all the technical and aerobic difficulties of the Confluence Trail. A good first ride from the nearby campground.

Land status: Canyonlands National Park, Needles District. The entrance fee is $10 per vehicle. Receipts are good for four days, and an annual pass is $50. Entrance fees to Canyonlands are good in all districts.

Map: USGS The Loop.

Finding the trailhead: From Center Street in Moab, drive 42.6 miles south on U.S. Highway 191 to the well-signed junction with Utah Highway 211, and turn right. Stay on this paved road for 38 miles, all the way to the entrance gate, and pay the fee. Park at the visitor center, which is also the trailhead. Allow time on the drive to visit Newspaper Rock. This pullout on the road into Canyonlands is a primo rock/art site.

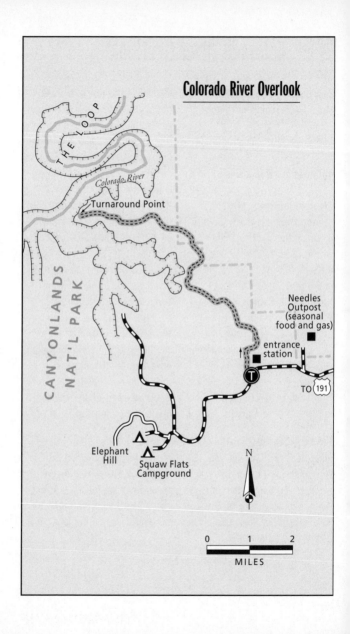

Colorado River Overlook

THE LOOP

Colorado River

Turnaround Point

CANYONLANDS NAT'L PARK

Needles Outpost (seasonal food and gas)

entrance station

TO (191)

Elephant Hill

Squaw Flats Campground

N

0   1   2

MILES

The Ride

0.0 The four-wheel-drive trail leaves the north (left) side of the parking lot. The track immediately forks—follow the sign pointing left. The first 2 miles descend gradually into the head of Salt Creek.

2.7 Another fork; keep right. The left-hand trail leads to the Lower Jump and is definitely worth the 0.15-mile hike (no bikes, please) down. The main route begins a moderate climb north out of the Salt Creek drainage, then rolls west toward the Colorado.

7.3 Trail's end. Look down about 1,000 feet to see the waters of the Colorado River rolling out of an enormous oxbow known as The Loop. From here the river flows about 4 miles to the confluence with the Green River (see Ride 23).

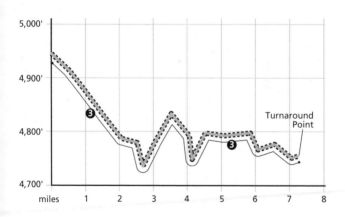

23 Confluence Overlook

Location: 70 miles south of Moab in Canyonlands National Park.

Distance: 15.3-mile lariat-shaped loop.

Approximate riding time: 3 to 5 hours plus at least an hour for the hike and gaping.

Physical difficulty: Strenuous. The initial climb saps your strength, then the sand finishes you off.

Technical difficulty: Moderate to challenging. Once ridden, Elephant Hill is never forgotten. Good sand skills are a big plus for this journey.

Trail surface: 15.3 miles on four-wheel-drive road. It starts off with rock steps up Elephant Hill, then gets sandy heading down Devil's Lane.

Highlights: Okay, so it sounds tiring and tough. It is. But the payoff—a short hike to see the confluence of the Green and Color-Red-Oh! Rivers—is worth the effort. When the rivers run true to their names, the mixing of color is spectacular. Bring a lock to secure your bike while hiking. Also use chain lube tha sets up dry to minimize sand damage. And bring some cash for the park entrance fee of $10.

Land status: Canyonlands National Park, Needles District. The entrance fee is $10 per vehicle. Receipts are good for four days and an annual pass is $50. Fees are good for all Canyonlands districts.

Map: USGS The Loop.

Finding the trailhead: From Center Street in Moab, drive 42.6 miles south on U.S. Highway 191 to the well-signed junction with Utah Highway 211 and turn right. Go west 38 miles on this paved road all the way to the entrance gate and Needles District visitor center, and pay the fee. From the visitor center continue 2.7 miles west on Utah 211, and turn left toward Squaw Flat Campground. Keep right twice to the gravel road to Elephant Hill. The trailhead parking area is 5.7 miles from the visitor center. Allow time on the drive in to

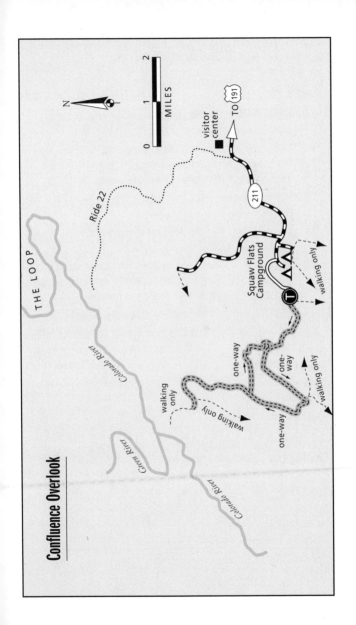

Confluence Overlook

THE LOOP

Green River

Colorado River

Colorado River

Ride 22

visitor center

TO 191

211

Squaw Flats Campground

walking only

one-way

one-way

one-way

walking only

walking only

N

MILES
0   1   2

visit Newspaper Rock. This rock/art site along the road into Canyon-lands will help set the mood for the ride ahead.

The Ride

0.0 Elephant Hill. You'll never forget the rock ledges and crags amongst the sand. It gets ya' comin' and goin'.

1.5 Turn left onto the one-way road (it's one-way for bikers, too). The sounds you've been hearing are the gasps of disbelief as your brain tries to take in the surroundings.

2.0 After crossing the wash, bear left and head into Devil's Pocket.

3.4 Turn right away from the Devil's Kitchen campsite and down toward Devil's Lane.

4.0 Turn right onto Devil's Lane, and follow it straight through sand hell. Sing along with the Steve Miller Band: "You've got to go through hell before you . . . get to heaven."

5.4 Keep left, and pass the one-way road home going right.

7.8 Keep right, and whirl past Cyclone Canyon to the end of the road.

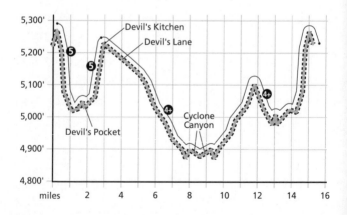

► And what a world of grandeur is spread before us! Below is the canyon through which the Colorado runs. We trace its course for miles, and at points catch glimpses of the river. From the northwest comes the Green in a narrow winding that seems bottomless from where we stand. Away to the west are lines of cliffs and ledges of rock—not such ledges as the reader may have seen where the quarryman splits his blocks, but ledges from which the gods might quarry mountains that, rolled out on the plain below, would stand a lofty range; and not such cliffs as the reader may have seen where the swallow builds its nest, but cliffs where the eagle is lost to view ere he reaches the summit.

Between us and the distant cliffs are the strangely carved and pinnacled rocks of the Toom'pin wunear' Tuweap'. On the summit of the opposite wall of the canyon are rock forms that we do not understand. Away to the east a group of eruptive mountains are seen—the Sierra la Sal, which we first saw two days ago through the canon of the Grand. Their slopes are covered with pines, and deep gulches are flanked with great crags, and snow fields are seen near the summits. So the mountains are in uniform—green, gray, and silver. Wherever we look there is but a wilderness of rocks—deep gorges where the rivers are lost below cliffs and towers and pinnacles, and ten thousand strangely carved forms in every direction, and beyond them mountains blending with the clouds.

—John Wesley Powell

8.6 This parking area means it's time to dismount. Park rangers say it's okay to lock bikes to the hitching post or gently to a juniper. Cable locks work, but the Krypto-style won't. Hike 1 mile from here to the confluence overlook. The hike mileage is not included in the odometer readings. After enjoying the world of grandeur, walk back, remount, and begin the journey back to civilization.

9.4 Turn left, retracing the route past Cyclone Canyon.

11.8 Turn left on the one-way road (see mile 5.4 above).

13.8 Turn left and head back over Elephant Hill. Unless you want to do another lap.

15.3 This epic ride is complete.

24 Pritchett Arch to Gatherer's Canyon

Location: 5 miles west of Moab.
Distance: 11.8-mile loop plus a portage.
Approximate riding time: 2 to 3 hours.
Physical difficulty: Moderately strenuous. There is one strenuous portion either way you ride this. But the majority is moderate.
Technical difficulty: Challenging. White Knuckle Hill rates as an extremely challenging climb and is only slightly easier as a descent. The more of the single-track that is ridden, the higher its rating.
Trail surface: 1.9 miles on gravel road; 8.9 miles on four-wheel-drive road; 1 mile on singletrack. The initial ride into Pritchett Canyon consists of sand and cobblestone. Some slickrock snacks await, as well as ledgy climbs and loose, eroded steeps.
Highlights: Pritchett Canyon, lined with cottonwoods, winds between towering sandstone walls through a region beset with geologic wonders and prehistoric relics. It costs a buck ($1.00) to access the trail. Technical treasures lie in wait beneath a picturesque veil for riders to discover. Tears of joy will flow when you think back on every facet of this jewel.
Land status: BLM. The first 200 yards crosses private property. The owner requires a $1.00 toll.
Maps: USGS Moab, Through Springs.

Finding the trailhead: From Center Street in Moab, drive 0.7 mile south on U.S. Highway 191 to Kane Creek Boulevard, and turn right between the Star Diner and McDonald's. Go 0.8 mile and stay left through the "Dangerous Intersection" on Kane (it appears to be a left turn). About 5.5 miles from Center Street, look for the trailhead on the left. Additional parking is just up the road. Pay $1.00 per bike. To bike to the trailhead from town, go south on 100 West and turn right onto Williams Way. Go 4 blocks and turn left onto 500 West. Pedal

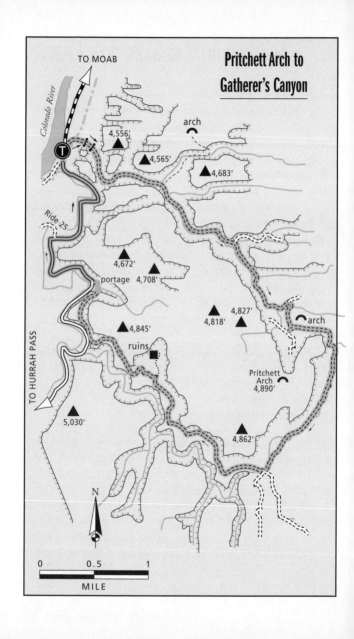

Pritchett Arch to Gatherer's Canyon

TO MOAB

Colorado River

T

arch

4,556'

4,565'

4,683'

Ride 25

4,672'

portage 4,708'

4,827'

4,818'

4,845'

arch

ruins

Pritchett Arch
4,890'

TO HURRAH PASS

5,030'

4,862'

N

0   0.5   1

MILE

0.4 mile to Kane Boulevard. Turn right and go 4.1 miles to the trail-head. This way is shorter and sees less traffic.

The Ride

0.0   After paying the toll, continue up the road past the private campground and through the gate.

0.2   Beware a technically challenging drop when starting through this sheer-walled canyon. There's a moderate-to-challenging bypass on the left.

0.4   Choose between a 2-foot hop up onto slickrock or the ramp on the right. Up ahead lie some skull-size stones (aka baby-heads) in a bed of sand.

1.6   Stay left and cross the technically challenging wash to continue up the canyon.

2.0   After another rocky spot the trail heads up a steep, technical grade.

2.4   The trail forks; turn right and continue up the same canyon.

2.9   Steep uphill with a technically moderate-to-challenging move.

3.0   Keep left as the trail splits then rejoins.

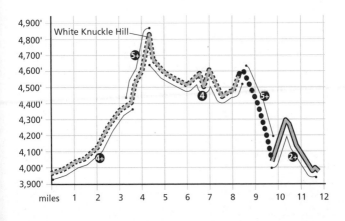

3.2 Rock patch of 30 yards (moderate-to-challenging).

3.5 Pedal into an open area, then right. Look for a road that heads up out of the wash on the right. It's easy to miss. If you end up riding on slickrock in the wash, you've gone too far. The steep eroded road is on the right and climbs sharply to look over the open area.

3.9 The track forks; go right (moderate-to-challenging).

4.0 Have a gander at Pritchett Arch, and turn left at this fork to continue. Surprise! There's another arch from whence the road came.

4.2 Keep right and head up the canyon.

4.4 The view from this bench is worth stopping for if you made it up without pushing. This is White Knuckle Hill, accurately named by jeepers.

5.7 The route passes spur roads to Pritchett Arch on the right.

6.1 Standing at the crossroads. Turn right. Straight heads to Kane Canyon Rim and is the return loop option for the Behind the Rocks Trail (Ride 18), which lies to the left.

7.0 The tread is ledgy, broken rock.

8.2 The track forks; go left. Right heads to an archaeological site.

8.5 Start the singletrack, and follow cairns around the cliff side. A good portion is rideable, but portage places occur frequently. When above the creek in Gatherer Canyon, keep following the cairns while looking for the most environmentally friendly way down. This area has taken abuse from people picking their own path. Please be patient, and follow the cairn-marked trail.

9.5 Turn right onto Kane Creek Boulevard (aka Hurrah Pass Road), climb this lovely hill, then coast back to the car.

11.8 Trailhead.

25 Amasa Back

Location: 5 miles west of Moab.
Distance: 11.2-mile out-and-back or 8.4-mile loop.
Approximate riding time: 2 hours.
Physical difficulty: Strenuous. The initial climb and especially the final climb back out are steep. Once on top, the route becomes fairly moderate.
Technical difficulty: Moderate to challenging. The first descent is very technical, and the climb up the other side tosses in some tough spots. Once on top there's a bit of smooth riding. But the whole route demands attention.
Trail surface: 2.4 miles on gravel road; 8.6 miles on four-wheel-drive road. The four-wheel-drive road has slickrock, dirt pack, and ledgy bedrock. The end of the route marks where the "self-exploration" of Amasa Back's expansive terrain begins.
Highlights: The insanely steep initial descent of this locals' favorite will test technical skills down and up while the following climb tests willpower. An extremely technical singletrack creates a loop option. Retracing the route downhill, however, is a rocky, fast-paced frolic. Life should be full of such choices.
Land status: BLM.
Maps: USGS Moab, Gold Bar Rim.

Finding the trailhead: From Center Street in Moab, drive 0.7 mile south on U.S. Highway 191 to Kane Creek Boulevard, and turn right between the Star Diner and McDonald's. Go 0.8 mile and stay left through a "Dangerous Intersection" on Kane (it appears to be a left turn). At 5.6 miles cross a cattleguard and look for the trailhead on the right. To bike to the trailhead from town, go south on 100 West and turn right onto Williams Way. Go 4 blocks and turn left onto 500 West. Pedal 0.4 mile to Kane Boulevard. Turn right and go 4.1 miles to the trailhead. This way is shorter and sees less traffic.

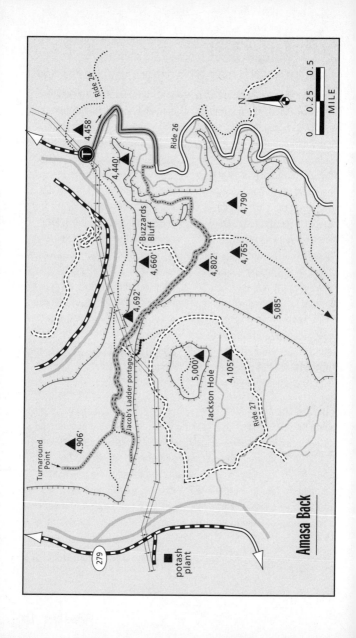

Ride 2A

4,458'

T

4,440'

Buzzards
Bluff

4,660'

4,692'

4,790'

4,765'

4,802'

5,085'

5,000'

Jackson Hole

4,105'

Ride 27

Jacob's Ladder portage

Ride 26

4,906'

Turnaround
Point

279

potash
plant

Amasa Back

N

0   0.25   0.5

MILE

The Ride

0.0 Take a right from the parking area and head up the dirt road.

1.2 The signed Amasa Back trail dives off the road to the right. Hang it out and grab the brakes for this Mr. Toad downhill!

1.3 A 3-foot drop! Careful.

1.4 The bottom of the initial descent can be confusing. The trail leads to a wash and immediately crosses over to begin the climb. It reaches an old gate in about 20 yards. Trails leading up and down the wash are not official. Hike them if you wish to explore.

1.7 Keep right and begin climbing through a series of switch-backs.

2.0 The respite from technical tests is over. Crank into moderate-to-challenging riding.

2.6 Stay right on the slickrock and continue climbing. Left is extremely technical and worth exploring for pioneer types as it eventually descends to mile 4.2 of the Hurrah Pass ride.

3.2 After reaching the ridge, the road descends to this fork. The main route stays left. Right is a 0.8-mile jaunt to Buzzards

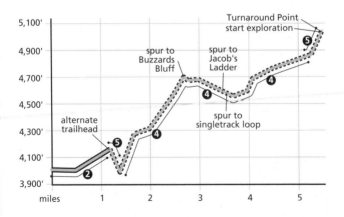

Bluff. It's sandy, but the view of the Colorado and Poison Spider Mesa is worth a look.

3.5   That's Jackson Hole off the cliff to the left. Two significant drops in the next 0.1 mile each earn a technical rating of challenging. The second drop has a moderate-to-challenging route, but it runs precariously close to the cliff's edge.

4.0   Keep on the main road through the next two spurs. The first leads left to Jacob's Ladder (see Ride 27). The second is a loop option for this ride. It's technically challenging and deposits riders in Kane Creek, not far from the trailhead.

4.2   Another supremely technical (moderate to challenging) spot. A road to the left offers an easier way up and rejoins above this section.

4.5   Switchback to the right here to go over the slickrock ridge.

4.7   Pretty technical from here on. The trail forks. Right leads to a lone petroglyph then becomes "pick your own." Or go left, and try to spot the cairns as the road grows faint and hard to follow. If you lose the trail, stay on slickrock and work up to the rim.

5.6   The rim. The overlook provides views of Jackson's Hole and the Potash plant. The Jug Handle ride (Ride 32) is visible as it starts along the river. To explore the expansive Amasa Back portion of this rock, return to mile 4.7 and wander along the other fork. See if you can find the petroglyph, but don't crush the cryptobiotic crust. Ride only on the rock. When you are finished exploring, retrace the route home.

26 Hurrah Pass

Location: 5 miles west of Moab on Kane Creek Boulevard.

Distance: 19.4-mile out-and-back or 29.6 miles when ridden from Moab.

Approximate riding time: 2 to 4 hours.

Physical difficulty: Moderate. Two climbs on the way out and one coming back are strenuous. Good climbers will find this easy, and non-climbers will swear it's strenuous.

Technical difficulty: Moderate. Tight corners can be tricky at speed, and the rocky sections occur on steeps.

Trail surface: 19.4 miles on gravel road.

Highlights: Hurrah Pass offers mild terrain under the tires amidst dramatic canyon scenery. The route runs beneath Hatch Point and the rim of Kane Springs Canyon, then clings to the side of the canyon as it winds up to the notch that is Hurrah Pass. From this vantage point Canyonlands National Park and the Colorado River are seen dissolving into the southwest, while the evaporative ponds of the nearby potash plant are reminders of the outside world in a land of solitude. Dead Horse Point and Island in the Sky rise farther to the west with the Jug Handle loop (Ride 32) just across the river. The Jackson Hole, Lockhart Canyon, and Chicken Corners routes (see Rides 27 and 28) continue over the pass.

Land status: State land and BLM.

Maps: USGS Moab, Trough Springs Canyon.

Finding the trailhead: From Center Street in Moab, drive 0.7 mile south on U.S. Highway 191 to Kane Creek Boulevard and turn right. The turn is just before McDonald's. Go 0.8 mile, and stay left through this "Dangerous Intersection" on Kane (it seems like a left turn). The trailhead is on the right just after a cattleguard and where the road turns to dirt at mile 5.6. To bike to the trailhead from town, go south

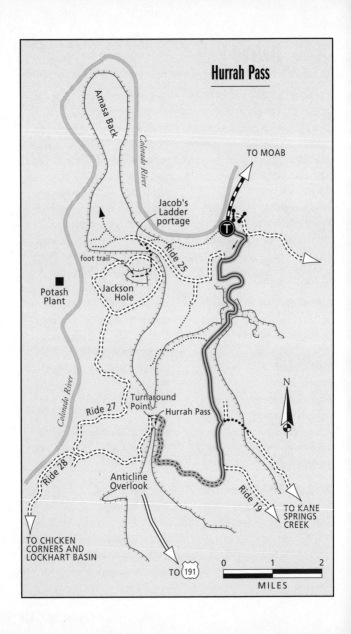

Hurrah Pass

Amasa Back

Colorado River

TO MOAB

T

Jacob's
Ladder portage

Ride 25

foot trail

Jackson
Hole

Potash
Plant

Colorado River

Ride 27

Turnaround
Point
Hurrah Pass

Ride 28

Anticline
Overlook

Ride 19

TO KANE
SPRINGS
CREEK

TO CHICKEN
CORNERS AND
LOCKHART BASIN

TO 191

N

0   1   2
MILES

on 100 West and turn right onto Williams Way. Go 4 blocks, and turn left onto 500 West. Pedal 0.4 mile to Kane Boulevard. Turn right, and go 4.1 miles to the trailhead. This latter way is shorter, sees less traffic, and makes the "Dangerous Intersection" slightly safer.

The Ride

0.0 From the parking area turn right and head up the dirt road.

1.2 Amasa Back Trail departs to the right. About 200 feet up on the right is a large cube of rock with petroglyphs on each side. The canyon below here also has many samples of rock art.

1.6 The hill tops out and begins a fast descent with a couple of sharp hairpin turns.

2.2 A reliable spring drips off the left canyon wall.

2.3 Gatherer's Canyon heads off to the left. It is the portage point of the Pritchett Canyon route (Ride 24).

3.2 Alternate trailhead parking.

4.2 Keep left as a spur right heads up an extremely technical mine road. True explorer types use this as a return from an

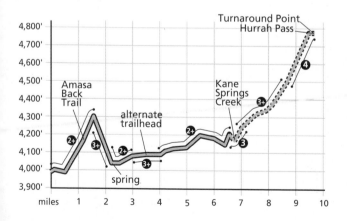

Amasa spur (Ride 25). The upcoming spurs on the left head to old mines. Stay on the main road.

6.4 The road crosses the sandy bed of Kane Springs Creek.

6.7 Stay on the main road as the Kane Springs jeep road leaves to the left (see Ride 19).

8.4 The climb turns tight corners and gets steeper and more technical. The right-hand spurs lead to overlooks of the valley just traveled in.

9.5 When you cross a cattleguard, you'll know the top is near.

9.7 Hurrah Pass summit. Passengers who aren't continuing to Chicken Corners, Jackson's Hole, Lockhart Basin, or any points between should retrace the route home.

19.4 Back at the trailhead.

27 Jackson Hole

Location: 5 miles west of Moab.

Distance: 22.5-mile loop.

Approximate riding time: 3.5 to 6 hours.

Physical difficulty: Strenuous. There are some downright painful hills on this jaunt, and the Jacob's Ladder portage is like backpacking a bike up a skyscraper in a cramped stairwell. Amasa Back adds two more hill climbs, the last of which is *very* steep.

Technical difficulty: Moderate to challenging. The ride to Jacob's Ladder isn't overly technical. The shake, rattle, and roll downhill from Hurrah Pass is jarring, and Jackson Hole is sandy. Amasa Back demands a lot of off-the-saddle riding.

Trail surface: 7.6 miles on gravel road; about 14.9 miles on four-wheel-drive road; plus a portage. The tread is pretty smooth up to Hurrah Pass, but then bedrock drops and cobblestones show up

on the other side. The Jackson Hole portion mixes sand and broken rock. The rock gets smoother on Amasa Back but is still ledgy.

Highlights: Jackson's Not-Hole and Amasa Rock dwarf bikers as they attack painful climbs and sandy washes spaced among mushroom-like rock formations in the old riverbed. At one point the trail sneaks beneath a gargoy-lesque passage of rock in Jackson Hole, which was once the path of the Colorado River. The portage up Jacob's Ladder has riders zombie-stepping up 400 feet on a narrow winding path made of packed rocks. The back-side of Hurrah Pass is a fast, bone-jarring, white-knuckle descent, and Amasa Rock offers still more downhill choices. A great day of riding!

Land status: State of Utah and BLM.

Maps: USGS Through Springs Canyon, Shafer Basin, Gold Bar Canyon, Moab.

Finding the trailhead: From Center Street in Moab, drive 0.7 mile south on U.S. Highway 191 to Kane Creek Boulevard, and turn right just before the McDonald's. Go 0.8 mile, and stay left through this

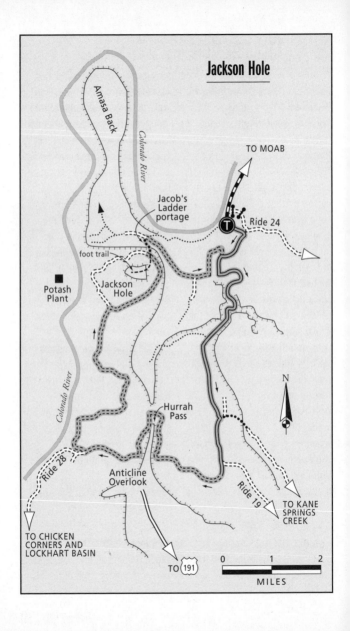

Jackson Hole

Amasa Back

Colorado River

TO MOAB

Jacob's Ladder portage

Ride 24

foot trail

Jackson Hole

Potash Plant

Colorado River

Hurrah Pass

N

Ride 28

Anticline Overlook

Ride 19

TO KANE SPRINGS CREEK

TO CHICKEN CORNERS AND LOCKHART BASIN

TO 191

0   1   2

MILES

"Dangerous Intersection" on Kane (it appears to be a left turn). About 5.6 miles from Center Street, look for the trailhead on the right just after a cattleguard where the road turns to dirt. To bike to the trailhead from town, go south on 100 West and turn right onto Williams Way. Go 4 blocks and turn left onto 500 West. Pedal 0.4 mile to Kane Boulevard. Turn right and go 4.1 miles to the trailhead. This way is shorter and sees less traffic. Epic.

The Ride

0.0 From the parking area turn right onto the gravel road.

1.2 Amasa Back Trail dives off to the right. A rock cube just ahead on the right is covered with petroglyphs.

1.6 The hill tops out and begins a fast descent with a couple of sharp hairpin turns.

2.2 A reliable spring drips off the left canyon wall.

2.3 Gatherer's Canyon heads off to the left. It is the portage point of the Pritchett Canyon route (Ride 24).

3.2 Alternate trailhead parking.

4.2 Keep left as a spur right heads up an extremely technical mine road. True explorer types use this as a return from an

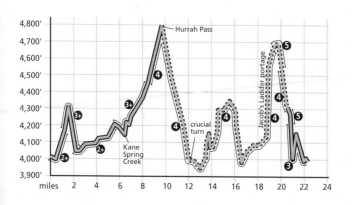

Amasa spur (Ride 25). The upcoming spurs on the left head to old mines. Stay on the main road.

6.4   The road crosses the sandy bed of Kane Springs Creek.

6.7   Stay on the main road as the Kane Springs jeep road leaves to the left (see Ride 19).

8.4   The climb turns tight corners and gets steeper and more technical. The right-hand spurs lead to overlooks of the valley just traveled in.

9.5   When you cross a cattleguard, you'll know the top is near.

9.7   Hurrah Pass. Point the tires downhill and hang on. Some rock ledges await, followed by intestine-shaking tread.

12.1   Turn right onto the faint trail in the wash. If you start climbing again after the lengthy downhill, you passed it. The trail leaves the wash on the right and is usually marked with a cairn. At speed, however, it's easy to zoom past. This paired with the fact that over the next rise another road goes right causes a lot of unplanned exploring. If you go up at all before turning, you missed it.

12.2   The track becomes extremely sandy for 0.2 mile.

12.8   Return of the sand monster.

12.9   The sand ends abruptly. Climb the eroding wall ahead.

13.4   "Return of the Wall" consists of chipped blocks of rock.

13.7   These gargoylesque rocks overlook a nice, relaxing stretch.

14.0   "Beneath the Planet Wall" (Wall III). More loose, chipped rock.

14.5   This sandy turn grasps at wheels.

16.6   *Crucial turn.* Turn back to the right and out of this wash. The road continues ahead, but it's longer and sandier. If you don't believe me, make sure to loop around the monolithic rock (which I've taken the liberty of calling Jackson's Not-Hole).

17.9   Careful on this wash crossing. It's steep and deep.

18.4   Turn right onto this spur.

18.6 Rig up for Jacob's Ladder. Odometer off.

18.6 Odometer back on at the top of Jacob's Ladder. Follow the road under the power lines away from the edge.

18.8 T intersection; turn right. See Amasa Back, Ride 25 (mile 4.0), for a singletrack option.

19.7 A spur goes left; stay right.

19.8 Downhill! Check out the La Sals looming over the Behind the Rocks fins and the arch to the southeast.

21.1 Cross the frequently wet wash and resume the trail up to the left on the opposite bank. Here comes a steep, technical slap in the face.

21.3 Turn right onto Kane Creek Boulevard (aka Hurrah Pass Road).

22.5 Done.

28 Chicken Corners

Location: 5 miles west of Moab.
Distance: 42-mile out-and-back.
Approximate riding time: 4 to 6 hours.
Physical difficulty: Strenuous. The ride features three solid climbs, but the main reason for this rating is the overall length.
Technical difficulty: Moderate. The downhills are fast with a few ledges and tight corners that demand respect!
Trail surface: 19.4 miles on gravel road; 22.6 miles on four-wheel-drive road. The downside of Hurrah Pass starts with bedrock drops followed by craggy cobblestones. Farther down, the road crosses several rough washes.

Highlights: Rumor has it that this ride's name stems from guides who enjoyed scaring people around the turns that skirt cliffs above the Colorado River. Thanks to our wonderfully protective government, the road has been "fixed" to give more room. Up close views of Pyramid Butte and into Canyonlands National Park are great. This is a long affair, so plan accordingly. Lockhart Basin, a multiday bike adventure, is accessed from this route.
Land status: BLM.
Maps: USGS Moab, Trough Spring Canyon, Shafer Basin.

Finding the trailhead: From Center Street in Moab, go 0.7 mile south on U.S. Highway 191 to Kane Creek Boulevard, and turn right. The turn is between the Star Diner and McDonald's. Go 0.8 mile, and stay left through a "Dangerous Intersection" to stay on Kane (it seems like a left turn). About 5.6 miles from Center Street, look for the trailhead on the right just after a cattleguard where the road turns to dirt. To bike to the trailhead from town, go south on 100 West and turn right onto Williams Way. Go 4 blocks and turn left onto 500 West. Pedal 0.4 mile to Kane Boulevard. Turn right and go 4.1 miles to the trailhead. This way is shorter and sees less traffic. Alternate parking is available for the next few miles (which cuts off the first—and last—hill).

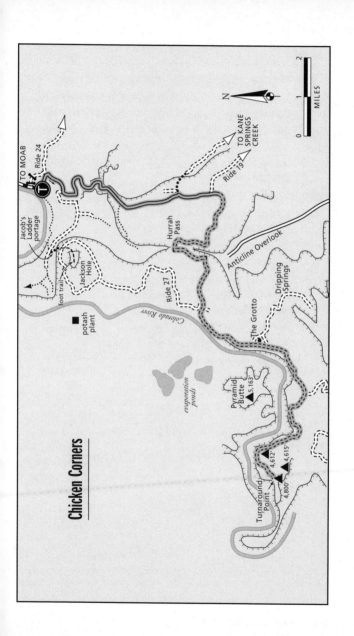

Chicken Corners

TO MOAB
Ride 24

Jacob's Ladder portage

Jackson Hole

foot trail

potash plant

Colorado River

evaporation ponds

Ride 27

Hurrah Pass

Anticline Overlook

The Grotto

Dripping Springs

TO KANE SPRINGS CREEK

Ride 19

Pyramid Butte ▲ 5,163

▲ 4,612

Turnaround Point

▲ 4,615

▲ 4,800

N

MILES
0   1   2

The Ride

0.0 From the parking area, head up the dirt road to Hurrah Pass.

1.2 Amasa Back Trail departs to the right. About 200 feet up on the right is a large cube of rock with petroglyphs on each side. The canyon below here also has many samples of rock art.

1.6 The hill tops out and begins a fast descent with a couple of sharp hairpin turns.

2.2 A reliable spring drips off the left canyon wall.

2.3 Gatherer's Canyon heads off to the left. It is the portage point of the Pritchett Canyon route (Ride 24).

3.2 Alternate trailhead parking.

4.2 Keep left as a spur right heads up an extremely technical mine road. True explorer types use this as a return from an Amasa spur (Ride 25). The upcoming spurs on the left head to old mines. Stay on the main road.

6.4 The road crosses the sandy bed of Kane Springs Creek.

6.7 Stay on the main road as the Kane Springs jeep road leaves to the left (see Ride 19).

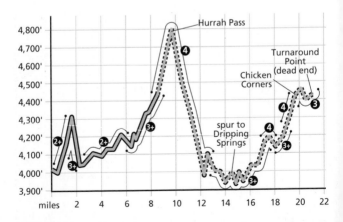

8.4 The climb turns tight corners and gets steeper and more technical. The right-hand spurs lead to overlooks of the valley just traveled in.

9.5 When you cross a cattleguard, you'll know the top is near.

9.7 Hurrah Pass. Head down the back side of the pass. Enjoy this adrenaline-infused, arm-numbing descent full of ledges and cobblestones.

12.1 Keep on the main road as the descent bottoms out where the Jackson Hole route (Ride 27) turns right.

12.2 After climbing from the Jackson turn, the road immediately descends again. When it hits the wash, look for a road scraped out of bare bedrock climbing to the right. Take this road. Missing this turn adds some sand, but it reconnects farther down the line.

12.5 The road turns left to avoid dropping off into the Colorado River below. As the ride progresses the river will be about 500 feet straight down.

14.2 Keep right as the spur to Dripping Springs goes left. Also on the right is Pyramid Butte, across the Colorado. From the right angle, it looks like something right outta Egypt.

16.5 Stay right past the road to Lockhart Basin, a nice, multiday ride that doesn't require permits.

19.6 This is where the road gets purdy darn skinny. Are you chicken?

21.0 Chicken Corners interruptus. After skirting around the skinny corners that gave the trail its name, the road finally comes to a dead end. Turn around and find a rhythm for the return grunt.

29 Moab Rim

Location: 2 miles west of Moab on Kane Creek Boulevard.
Distance: 12.4-mile out-and-back.
Approximate riding time: 2 hours.
Physical difficulty: Strenuous. The initial climb, which rises 900 feet in under 1 mile, is rideable—honest. On top, the terrain is much gentler. When ridden as a clockwise loop, this route is moderate with a long, tedious portage.
Technical difficulty: Challenging. This is actually a moderate-to-challenging ride sandwiched between two extremely challenging patches. The climb and descent to and from the rim are extremely technical and steep. The slickrock steps are unforgiving both up and down, but who needs forgiveness?
Trail surface: 10 miles on four-wheel-drive road; 2.4 miles on singletrack (half that if shuttling or doing a loop). It's amazing that four-wheelers can drive this trail! It consists of slickrock, slickrock steps, and some sandy stretches. If ridden as a loop, the

hidden valley portion that heads through a rockslide is rideable only by an elite handful; it's a portage for the rest of us.
Highlights: Scenery steals the show—massive hunks of sandstone boil up through the desert and Moab simulate a scenic flight over town. The difficult sections will have techies drooling while hopping up and diving down. Moab Rim can be ridden as a loop either direction or as an out-and-back to avoid the portage. I suggest the out-and-back. The option of linking this ride to Beneath the Wires (Ride 30) is fun, too. October's Fat Tire Fest includes a variety of events on the slickrock road to the rim; both uphill and down.

Ever wish for a ski lift to lug you and your trusty mount up to the top? Then the Moab Rim Adventure Park is just what you asked for! You can get to the top of Moab Rim for $10 without turning a pedal, and $26 gives you a full day of lifts. New trails take advantage of the park's private property and then funnel riders back onto the established

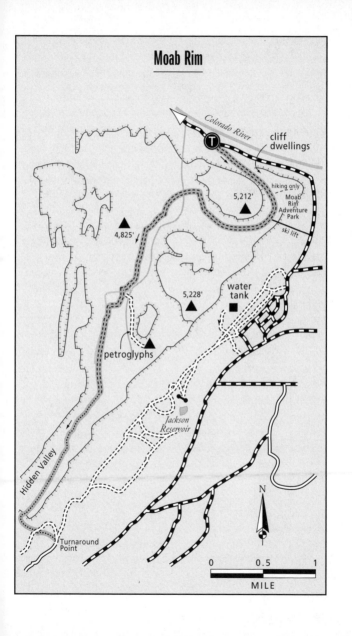

Moab Rim

Colorado River

cliff
dwellings

T

5,212'

hiking only

Moab
Rim
Adventure
Park

ski lift

4,825'

5,228'

water
tank

petroglyphs

*Jackson
Reservoir*

Hidden Valley

Turnaround
Point

N

0   0.5   1

MILE

road through the BLM land. The goal is for a borderless playground for your full-suspension steed. A map to the park is available with your lift ticket. The park, formerly called the Moab Skyway, is located on Kane Creek Boulevard 1 mile from Main Street. **Land status:** BLM. **Map:** USGS Moab.

Finding the trailhead: From Center Street in Moab, travel 0.7 mile south on U.S. Highway 191 to Kane Creek Boulevard, and turn right. The turn is just before McDonald's. Go 0.8 mile, and stay left through this "Dangerous Intersection" on Kane (it appears to be a left turn). About 3.5 miles from Center Street (2.8 miles from McDonald's), look for the trailhead on the left. To bike to the trailhead from town, go south on 100 West and turn right onto Williams Way. Go 4 blocks and turn left onto 500 West. Pedal 0.4 mile to Kane Boulevard. Turn right, and go 2.7 miles to the trailhead. This way is shorter and sees less traffic.

The Ride

0.0 From the trailhead registration box, follow the "road" up the slickrock ramp.

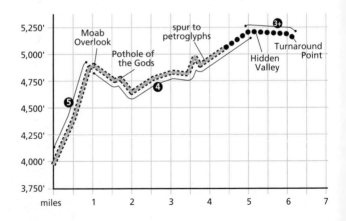

0.4 Swing around a quick switchback here as the rock runs out. Pick up the road again on the next fin.

0.9 Up on top. That was the tough part! Walk to the edge, and enjoy the view while catching your breath or administering CPR to your riding partners.

1.1 The road forks; keep right. Left goes to another viewpoint.

1.6 Roll down and up the slickrock softened with sand. The orange sand is laced with black cryptobiotic crust. The huge rock formations are ancient sand dunes.

1.8 Keep right at this fork. Left is an extremely sandy route that is fun but not on a bike.

1.9 Cairns mark the way on the slickrock.

2.1 Slickrock play zone.

2.4 Go up and across the slickrock here.

2.7 Find a slickrock ramp down to the road.

2.9 Careful! A couple of technically moderate-to-challenging ledges pop up here.

3.5 The Low Road rejoins from the left.

3.7 The route stays right here. But petroglyphs await those who climb the road to the left.

4.4 The road ends but the route continues on singletrack. Follow it straight over the rock that seems to halt progress, then up moderate-to-challenging tread to the ridge.

4.6 The ridge. The trail becomes packed, smooth, and occasionally sandy.

6.2 The trail becomes unrideable. Portage down to the registration box below or turn back, retracing the route to the slickrock stairway back down to the Colorado River.

30 Beneath the Wires

Location: Moab.
Distance: 8-mile out-and-back.
Approximate riding time: 1 hour.
Physical difficulty: Moderate. Short steeps will strain the thighs, but this is such a short loop it doesn't warrant a strenuous rating.
Technical difficulty: Moderate. Erosion is the main obstacle here. Deep ruts cut across the road, forcing riders to keep awake.
Trail surface: 8 miles on four-wheel-drive road that consists of eroded clay and packed sediments. Don't ride this when it's wet!
Highlights: This is a great quick fix, with instant access from Moab. The route presents a surprising challenge both technically and physically while racing beneath Moab Rim on utility access roads. Lots of roads intertwine here for endless, roller-coaster variety. A couple of the spurs lead to private property, so please heed all signs. This ride links with the Hidden Valley trailhead portion of the Moab Rim Trail for a good loop option with a portage. A note: I felt a small buzz from my pedals while standing Beneath the Wires. Electrifying!
Land status: City of Moab, BLM, and private holdings.
Map: USGS Moab.

Finding the trailhead: Ride from downtown Moab. Visitors can park either at the visitor center at Main and Center Street or at the trailhead. To reach the trailhead, go 0.8 mile south on Main from Center Street and turn right onto Dogwood. Follow this road past the photo shop, and park on the road. If there isn't a spot to park, it's probably best to leave the car at your hotel/camp.

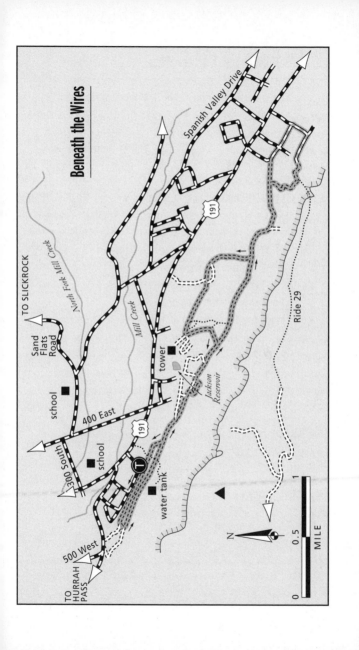

Beneath the Wires

TO SLICKROCK

North Fork Mill Creek

Sand Flats Road

school

Mill Creek

400 East

300 South

school

191

tower

Jackson Reservoir

191

water tank

500 West

TO HURRAH PASS

Ride 29

Spanish Valley Drive

N

MILE

0   0.5   1

The Ride

0.0 Ride up the dirt road that starts at the end of Dogwood and heads toward the water tower. It immediately runs into an intersection. Turn right, and stay on this road past the small spur trails at mile 0.2.

0.6 The road loops back upon itself to parallel the initial route. Stay on this road, and pick and chose routes with the map.

0.9 Pass by Stocks' Corral.

1.0 Go straight through this intersection.

1.2 Turn left or head straight. Right heads to the water tower. If turning left, turn right in 0.1 mile at the four-way intersection.

1.6 The left fork here is easier than the right.

1.8 Go right here to avoid trespassing.

1.9 Keep right through here. The far left is trespassing, and the middle road is insanely steep.

3.2 Note the road on the left for the roller-coaster return ride.

4.0 The Hidden Valley trailhead. This is the back entrance to the Moab Rim Trail. Turn around and reconnoiter a way back.

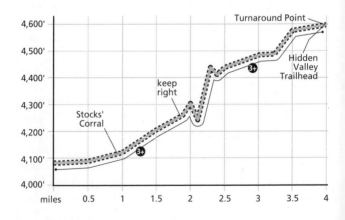

31 Poison Spider Mesa and the Portal Trail

Location: 10 miles west of Moab.

Distance: 12.9-mile loop via the Portal Trail or 12.8-mile out-and-back.

Approximate riding time: 2 to 4 hours.

Physical difficulty: Strenuous. The initial climb starts the muscle burn, the sand sucks any reserves, and the slickrock steeps finish the job. The upper body gets a workout with the technical sections, especially on the Portal Trail.

Technical difficulty: Challenging. Within its first 0.5 mile, the road turns technical with a loose-rock climb. Later, slickrock staircases pose extreme tests of ledging abilities. Sand and slickrock steeps complete the recipe for a classic ride. The icing on the cake is the Portal Trail, which is a technical and mental challenge. Some difficult moves occur where there is no room for error. Fall here, and you won't land for another 400 feet. Cyclists have died here.

Trail surface: 12.8 miles on four-wheel-drive road. While listed as four-wheel-drive road, a majority of this ride is anything but a road. When on slickrock it follows blazes painted on the rock. The Portal Trail loop option includes 2.5 miles of singletrack. This ride has a classic recipe: start with packed dirt. Add some ruts, loose rocks, sand, bedrock ledges, and slickrock. Mix well. For easier riding let soak in a good rain. For a looser, more difficult ride, do not add liquids. Use only premium-grade Moab slickrock.

Highlights: This famous must-do trail is a technical, physical, and mental workout. Views of the Behind the Rocks fins set against the La Sals are an obvious photo op, as is the arch. The slickrock is massive, the sand annoying, and The Portal is downright dangerous. Its narrowest portion is about 3 feet wide with a 400-foot drop on the left and a rock wall on the right. A technically challenging boulder hop on the skinniest part is avoidable by riding a 4-inch-wide patch of dirt directly on the cliff edge. A portage allows the wise to scramble past the exposed part. Unfortunately, the most technically difficult part of The Portal comes later. While not exposed it is still technically challenging all the way down. It too is walkable, but it ain't a pleasant stroll and can cause trouble for those still on their steeds. Walking the narrowest point of the Portal Trail is strongly advised.

Land status: BLM.

Maps: USGS Moab, Gold Bar Rim.

Finding the trailhead: From Center and Main in Moab, drive 4.3 miles north on U.S. Highway 191 to the Potash Road, Utah Highway 279. Travel west past the ruins, the Portal Trail's terminus, "Wallstreet," and the petroglyphs to the Dinosaur tracks sign at mile 10.4 that marks the trailhead. Go 0.1 mile up the dirt road to a parking area. Park here. The trailhead has a pit toilet and an information kiosk.

The Ride

0.0 Potash Road. Head up the gravel road. A BLM information display and parking are at the 0.1-mile mark. Most people will actually start riding at the 0.1 mark.

0.4 The road forks; stay right.

0.5 This technical spot is just an itty-bitty sample of what lies ahead.

0.9 This loose and steep hill looks much easier than it is . . . and it doesn't look *that* easy.

1.0 The road turns right and goes down briefly in a technically moderate-to-challenging move (but rank it challenging on the way back).

1.3 The road bends to the left and remains eroded and moderately technical.

1.4 Stay right past the faint spur here.

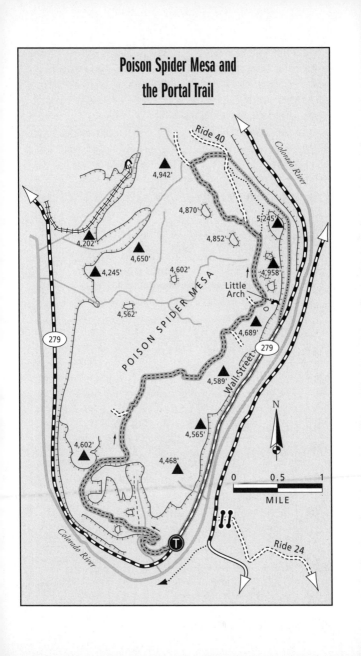

Poison Spider Mesa and the Portal Trail

Ride 40

Colorado River

▲ 4,942'

4,870'

5,245' ▲

4,852'

▲ 4,202'

▲ 4,650'

▲ 4,958'

▲ 4,245'

4,602'

Little Arch

P O I S O N   S P I D E R   M E S A

4,562'

4,689'

(279)

(279)

Wall Street

▲ 4,589'

N

▲ 4,565'

▲ 4,602'

▲ 4,468'

0   0.5   1

MILE

(T)

Colorado River

Ride 24

1.6 Another spur goes left; stay right.

2.1 The action gets fast and furious after the sand makes its entrance. Just ahead lies some brutal climbing, slickrock, more sand, and then some ledges for a barrage of moderate-to-challenging obstacles.

2.4 Mac-Daddy sand trap.

2.5 Go up this technically challenging patch of rock, then right at the fork to follow the painted white "jeeps" stenciled on the rock.

2.9 More sand, then more slickrock and a view of Behind the Rocks.

3.1 After this slickrock steep, go left at the fork following the painted diamond (the jeeps go right).

3.5 The trails rejoin and bear left.

3.6 Keep left at this slickrock transition for the easier (moderate-to-challenging) way up. Right is a technically challenging move.

3.9 Stay left here.

5.8 Ugh. Another monster sand trap.

6.0 The road forks; stay right.

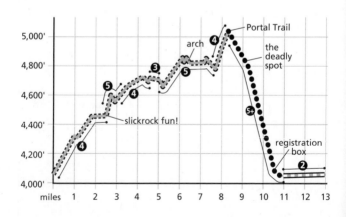

6.4 After a slickrock ascent, park the bikes, and head off to the right to see the arch. This is the spot to turn around if you're not riding the Portal Trail.

6.5 Back on the trail. The slickrock becomes a steep up-and-down roller coaster.

6.7 The track forks; stay left.

7.2 Go left up the slickrock wall. Then head for a low notch in the rock formations. Cairns and jeeps may point the way, but don't count on it. Simply head to the rock wall, and look for the notch through it. To the right is a sandy, hard-to-follow trail that eventually leads to The Portal. Left makes more sense.

7.7 The road becomes visible again then forks. Turn right and head back up the hill. It gets ledgy as it climbs to the rim.

8.3 Top. The Portal Trail goes right. Views here extend into Moab, the Slickrock Trail, Arches National Park, and the La Sals. This becomes a gathering area in busy times, like a ski area. Riders size up each other before heading down the Portal Trail.

9.3 Slow for the skinny spot that everyone talks about. If you have any doubt (sense?), carry your bike over this rock. The move itself wouldn't be too bad if it weren't for the 400-foot bunny hop on the outside. Even the best full suspension won't soften that landing. The hard part follows.

10.5 Read the comments in the trail registration box here. This is where everybody tries to think of a creative way to say that the Portal Trail was really neat.

10.8 The trail ends at the Potash Road. Turn right to return to the car. Beware the big trucks that roar down the road. They, too, have claimed a biker's life.

12.9 Turn right and climb up to the parking lot.

32 Jug Handle Loop–The Shafer Trail

Location: 18 miles west of Moab.

Distance: 36.5-mile loop.

Approximate riding time: 3 to 6 hours.

Physical difficulty: Strenuous. The climb up the Shafer Trail is major-league. It rises 1,240 feet in 3 miles, gaining 920 feet of that from mile 17 to 18.5.

Technical difficulty: Moderate. Most of this ride is free of major technical sections. But the drop through Pucker Pass in Long Canyon has some solid moderate-to-challenging riding and tight switchbacks that come up faster than lunch on a roller coaster.

Trail surface: 25.7 miles on gravel and four-wheel-drive roads; 10.8 miles on paved road. The gravel and four-wheel-drive roads are basically packed clay. When wet it's slicker than snot on a glass doorknob and is best

avoided. The upper portion of Long Canyon is rocky and eroded. The pavement is comparatively smooth, hard, and black, with white and yellow paint occurring in definite patterns.

Highlights: Making it to the top of the Shafer Trail is a rush for hammerheads, and the descent down Long Canyon will thrill downhillers. The trail climbs gradually through a dramatic, desolate landscape wrought with crumbling cliffs. At the White Rim the climb becomes a brutal slap in the face. Long Canyon features Pucker Pass, which requires a heads-up move on rough terrain before diving into the depths of the canyon below. Make sure your brakes are in top shape!

Land status: BLM and Canyonlands National Park.

Maps: USGS Shafer Basin, Musselman Arch, and The Knoll.

Finding the trailhead: From the visitor center in downtown Moab, drive 4.3 miles north onto U.S. Highway 191. Turn left onto Utah Highway 279 (Potash Road), and drive another 14.1 miles to a trailhead parking area immediately after the Jug Handle Arch on the right, across a set of railroad tracks. Both the arch and the parking

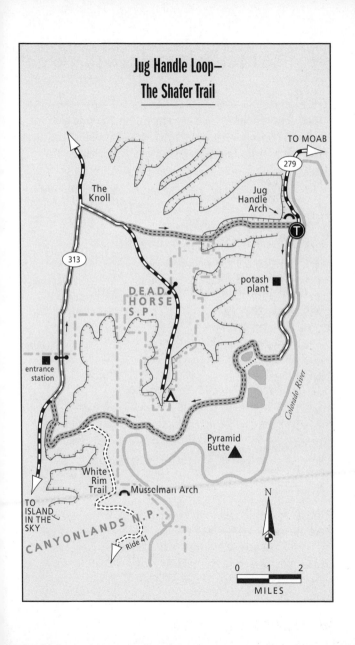

Jug Handle Loop–
The Shafer Trail

TO MOAB

279

The Knoll

Jug Handle Arch

313

T

potash plant

DEAD HORSE S.P.

entrance station

Colorado River

Pyramid Butte

White Rim Trail

Musselman Arch

TO ISLAND IN THE SKY

CANYONLANDS N.P.

Ride 41

N

0   1   2

MILES

area are signed. Potash Road also has signed archaeological and dinosaur points of interest en route to the parking area.

The Ride

0.0 From the parking area, turn right onto Potash Road and pedal south along the Colorado River.

1.7 Intersection. Go straight and pass the potash plant.

3.1 The road turns to dirt then begins to climb.

4.1 Top this hill and enjoy a brief downhill run, then grind up and over another rise.

5.2 Getting bored—washboard, that is!

8.5 Continue straight through this open area.

5.5 Currently the route goes straight through a four-way intersection. Obey the signs! The potash plant managers reroute traffic depending upon their evaporative needs.

9.2 A spur heads left to a Colorado River overlook. Pyramid Butte is now to stern.

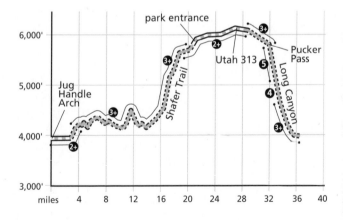

9.9 Keep on the main road here. The first spur right beats itself against the canyon wall. Another faint spur dead-ends to the left.

11.8 Keep right on the main road as it makes a sweeping 90-degree turn.

14.4 Through the wash and up. The going gets a bit technical ahead as the road weaves up the south fork of Shafer Canyon.

15.1 Relief is in sight (it's usually well supplied with toilet paper).

16.1 Turn right at the intersection in Shafer Camp, and enjoy the initial gradual climb. Left heads off to Musselman Arch on the White Rim Trail.

17.0 From this point most people awaken to what's ahead of them. Think motivational thoughts. Does it help to know that the climb tapers off in 1.9 miles after gaining 1,000 feet?

18.9 Yes, but it helps even more to know that a 1,000-foot elevation gain is behind you. Look off to the right to see the spaghetti-like road below. This is called The Neck. The bend in the Colorado is labeled Goose Neck.

21.4 After a much more mellow climb, the road meets The Island in the Sky Road inside Canyonlands National Park. Turn right and head out on this paved road.

27.3 Turn right here toward Dead Horse Point on Utah 313.

28.9 Bear left here onto the dirt road as Utah 313 veers right. The road is marked with a stop sign. Remain on this road, passing numerous spurs as it rolls through juniper highlands.

29.9 Stay right and rattle over washboards.

32.1 The road bends left and down, giving a view of Poison Spider Mesa, Behind the Rocks, and the La Sals before diving through Pucker Pass into Long Canyon.

35.5 Time to flex the hands. A mach-5 downhill tapers off for a relaxing finish to the car.

36.5 Trailhead.

33 Gemini Bridges

Location: 10 miles north of Moab.

Distance: 13.8-mile one-way with a shuttle. Some choose to start at the ride's end point for a 15.6-mile round-trip to the bridges.

Approximate riding time: 1.5 hours without sight-seeing time. Plan on a full day to explore.

Physical difficulty: Easy. It's all downhill except for a doozy of a climb at the end. The upper body takes a beating.

Technical difficulty: Moderate. Riding at high speed increases the degree of difficulty! The trail to Gemini Bridges is challenging in places.

Trail surface: 13.8 miles on gravel road with a few sections of four-wheel-drive track. The actual trail to Gemini Bridges is mostly on slickrock.

Highlights: Gemini Bridges (technically, they are arches) are twin spans over a deep canyon. Be careful when crossing them on a bike—a fall would be fatal. The route options here are staggering: Bull Canyon, Four Arches Trail, Arth's Pasture, Behind Goony Rock, and Beneath the Bridges are the common ones. Start early, take a topo map, and have fun exploring. Bike shops can help you arrange a shuttle to keep it all downhill. If you're quiet and lucky, you may be rewarded with a glimpse of the endangered desert sheep.

Land status: BLM.

Maps: USGS The Knoll, Gold Bar, and Klondike.

Finding the trailhead: From Center and Main in Moab, drive 10.2 miles north on U.S. Highway 191. Look for a gravel parking area on the left signed GEMINI BRIDGES. The turn is directly across the road from the MOAB CHUCKWAGON sign. This is the shuttle parking area (or an alternate trailhead for those who like climbing). For the main trailhead continue about 1.2 miles north on US 191 and turn left onto Utah Highway 313. Drive 12.8 miles west on Utah 313. Shortly after passing a pump station on the left, look for a gravel road on the left near the top of a hill. This is the trailhead.

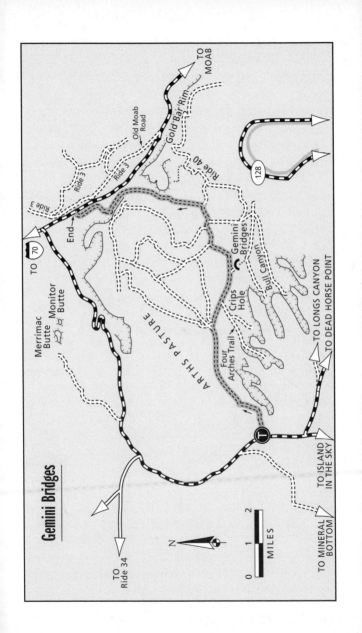

Gemini Bridges

N

MILES
0 1 2

Merrimac Butte
Monitor Butte

TO 70

Ride 3

Ride 3

Old Moab Road

Gold Bar Rim

TO MOAB

128

Ride 40

End

Gemini Bridges

ARTHS PASTURE

Crips Hole

Bull Canyon

Four Arches Trail

TO LONGS CANYON

TO DEAD HORSE POINT

TO ISLAND IN THE SKY

TO MINERAL BOTTOM

TO Ride 34

The Ride

0.0 Head down the gravel road and hang on as canyon views speed by on the right.

3.8 A four-wheel-drive track goes left to Arth's Pasture (see the optional route described below). Stay right.

4.0 Another track breaks left to Arth's Pasture. Stay right.

4.7 The Four Arches Trail into Crips Hole goes right (see optional route below). Stay straight on the main road.

5.8 A sign that says GEMINI BRIDGES points out this right turn. Gemini twins are painted on the slickrock to blaze the trail.

6.0 The arches . . . an awesome picnic site. When you're ready, retrace your tracks back to the main road.

6.2 Turn right onto the main road and continue the descent. Ignore the well-signed spurs and follow the twins.

7.5 The Arth's Pasture option (see below) returns on the left. Stay right.

8.3 Keep right as the other Arth's Pasture road joins up.

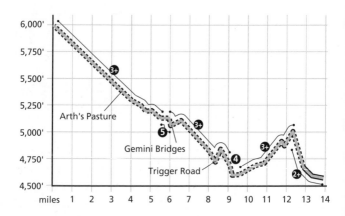

8.5 This is the crucial Trigger Road intersection for those who plan on exploring. Bull Canyon's two forks and Trigger's overlook of Day Canyon lie down this road to the left (see the optional route described below). Stay left to complete the ride described here.

9.1 Turn left after a steep, loose descent. Stay on this main road all the way to the trail's end.

10.8 The hill climb hath arrived.

12.3 After a false summit the real top makes the scene.

13.8 End of the line. Turn right into the parking area. If you didn't bring a car, follow the access directions back to the trailhead and have fun! It's also possible to link with Ride 3, Courthouse Wash, or pedal back down to town.

Arth's Pasture Option: At mile 3.8 or 4, turn left. Pedal 0.5 mile to a four-way intersection. Keep right, but don't turn back toward the main trail. Stay on this main road to make a huge arc north of the route described above. The 7.0-mile mark offers a choice: Left leads down a slickrock road that returns to the main route at its 8.3-mile point, while straight leads to the 7.5-mile point.

Four Arches Option: Turn right at mile 4.7 and drop into Crips Hole. Climb out of the wash, and stay right past a spur. Follow this road back into the box canyon, and look for the jug handle–type arches. If it didn't rain a few hours ago, this option will be extremely difficult due to deep sand.

Trigger Road Options: Trigger Road accesses Two Tortoise and Monticello Rocks, Bull Canyon beneath the Bridges, Bull Canyon's Dry Fork, and Day Canyon, all in that order. The first turn is a left, 1.4 miles from the main route. It heads to the Rocks and loops back to mile 9.1 in the main ride description above. On this road avoid the first left, then keep left at all remaining junctions to complete the loop. After the 1.4-mile point, the two Bull Canyon spurs come up in order. Passing these by leads to the dead end of Trigger Road, which overlooks Day Canyon.

34 Hey Joe Green Loop

Location: 26 miles northeast of Moab.

Distance: 33.4-mile loop plus a steep, technical 0.5-mile portage.

Approximate riding time: 4 to 6 hours.

Physical difficulty: Moderately strenuous. The hills are fairly gradual but slow-going. Sand, distance, and the portage add up to a physically draining ride.

Technical difficulty: Moderate. While the majority of the ride is in the moderate range, dropping into Spring Canyon is tricky and unforgiving, a moderate-to-challenging pitch. Keep momentum in the sand traps along the Green River. The portage is tough; it climbs steeply up slickrock and broken bedrock with a small degree of exposure.

Trail surface: 16.6 miles on gravel road; 16.8 miles on four-wheel-drive road; 0.5-mile portage. The gravel road has a few mild washboard sections. The four-wheel-drive descent into Spring Canyon is rocky, and the riverside is soft, rideable sand.

Highlights: This nice rolling road suddenly sprouts teeth as it rocks down into Spring Canyon in search of the river. The road is sandy but firm as it follows the Green River's twists between steep canyon walls. The route ducks in and out of gauntlets of tamarisk trees. The zombie-stepping, one-hand-free portage is a climb with some exposure that requires shoes with good soles. From the top it's a long, gradual ascending ride home.

Land status: BLM.

Maps: USGS Dubinky, Bow Knot, Tenmile Point.

Finding the trailhead: Set your car's trip odometer to 0.0 at Center Street in Moab, and drive 11.4 miles north on U.S. Highway 191. Turn left onto Utah Highway 313, and follow signs toward Dead Horse Point and Canyonlands. At mile 20.1 (8.7 miles from US 191), turn right onto Dubinky Well Road. This dirt road leaves Utah 313 after a

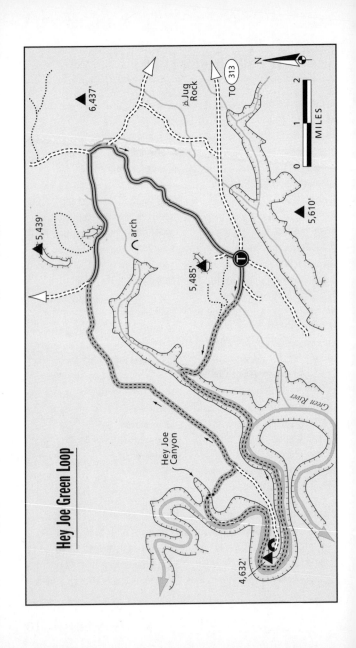

Hey Joe Green Loop

6,437'

TO 313

ᴚ Jug Rock

5,610'

5,439'

⌒ arch

5,485'

Green River

Hey Joe Canyon

4,632'

N

MILES
0 1 2

gradual left-hand bend. Stay on this main road, keeping left at the prominent spur at mile 21.7 that goes to Dubinky Well. Roll up to a four-way intersection at the top of a hill at mile 27.9. This is the trail-head.

The Ride

0.0 From the four-way intersection, continue in the original direction of travel, away from Utah 313. Remain on this road, avoiding all spurs.

3.4 This wash has a nasty drop. The road skirts the cliff side, then begins a wild, technical downhill.

4.6 The descent ends in this wash. Climb out to the right onto the road. Don't forget to look up at the canyon walls as you press on.

6.2 The road forks; turn right and begin heading upriver.

6.7 The big, rusty object on the right is an old ferry mooring.

7.4 The doubletrack is sandy and overgrown.

9.2 A technically moderate-to-challenging patch.

11.8 Race along the riverbank, then into tamarisk hollows.

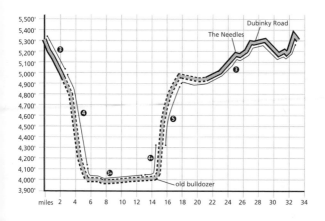

14.3 An old bulldozer marks a right-hand turn up into twisted Hey Joe Canyon and conjures images of Ed Abbey's *Monkey Wrench Gang*.

15.1 This climb gets rough, then skirts the Hey Joe Mine. Continue past the mine, then look for a trail to switchback farther up the canyon and above the mine. The best of the numerous trails heads upcanyon a ways before switching back to scramble up the bench. Rig up (shoulder your bike) and follow the cairns. This hair-raising portage twists up slickrock and broken rock and requires a free hand for balance. Falling here ain't healthy. A few spots ease off enough to be rideable, but this never lasts long.

15.5 A rusted gas tank marks the finish of the portage. This odometer reading is a good restarting point. The road ahead is flat and often sandy.

15.7 Turn left at a T intersection. Right heads to an arch.

16.7 Another T intersection; go left. A few spurs leave this road, but you stay on the main road. A rugged climb awaits before giving way to a gradual spin.

23.6 A road joins from the left, followed shortly by a gate. Please close the gate behind you.

25.2 The rock formation that looks like a person on his back with a foot stone is called The Needles. The next right-hand spur heads 1.7 miles to a tubelike arch formation.

27.2 Turn right onto the gravel road. To the left the road heads to Dubinky Well and then to Blue Hills Road. But right leads home.

27.7 The road forks; turn right for a gradual ascent to the trailhead. Dubinky Road continues left to rejoin the access road before Utah 313.

32.5 Turn left at a T intersection.

33.4 End the loop back at your car.

35 Monitor and Merrimac

Location: 16 miles north of Moab off of U.S. Highway 191.

Distance: 12.5-mile out-and-back with a small loop at the far end. Add 2.6 miles for the Courthouse Rock option and 1.5 miles for a side trip to Determination Towers.

Approximate riding time: 2 hours plus side trips and slickrock play time.

Physical difficulty: Moderate to strenuous. This ride is much easier after rain helps firm up the long, sandy stretches.

Technical difficulty: Moderate. The slickrock on the buttes can serve up challenging delights, but easier routes can be found. The road leading to the buttes is straightforward but sandy.

Trail surface: 3.2 miles on gravel road; 7 miles on four-wheel-drive road; 2.3 miles on slickrock.

Highlights: Monitor and Merrimac Buttes are named after the old Civil War ironside ships. Here

they fight in a sea of sand. History buffs will recognize their shapes instantly as the *Monitor* on the left and the *Merrimac* on the right. Both buttes offer slickrock playgrounds. Just be careful around abrupt areas of "not rock," also known as cliffs. Circumnavigating the "ships" requires a bit of mental work. No worries; be careful and the rest will roll into place. Optional side trips include Determination Towers, Tusher Canyon (Rides 36 and 37), and Courthouse Rock. Rumors of sand keep people away from this trail. The rumors are based in fact, but after a rain it becomes a pussycat. Without rain count on some pushing; during rain gooey mud makes the access tricky. Nevertheless, this is one of the region's classic rides.

Land status: BLM.

Maps: USGS Merrimac, Jug Handle.

Finding the trailhead: From the intersection of Center and Main in Moab, drive 16.5 miles north on US 191. Turn left onto Mill Canyon Road, and cross the railroad tracks. It comes up rather quickly. Just

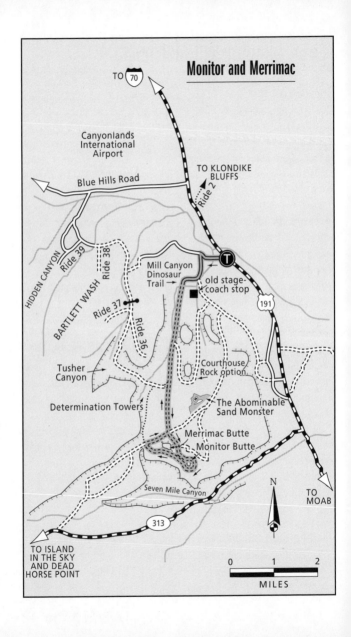

Monitor and Merrimac

TO 70

Canyonlands International Airport

Blue Hills Road

TO KLONDIKE BLUFFS
Ride 2

HIDDEN CANYON
Ride 39

Ride 38

BARTLETT WASH

Ride 37

Ride 36

Mill Canyon Dinosaur Trail

old stage-coach stop

191

Courthouse Rock option

Tusher Canyon

The Abominable Sand Monster

Determination Towers

Merrimac Butte
Monitor Butte

Seven Mile Canyon

N

313

TO MOAB

TO ISLAND IN THE SKY AND DEAD HORSE POINT

0   1   2

MILES

look for the railroad to get really close to the road. Then, after mile marker 141, look for a small MILL CANYON ROAD sign marking the ramp up to the railroad tracks. Don't be fooled by the prominent No Trespassing sign. It pertains only to the railroad corridor. Either park across the tracks, or follow this road downhill 0.2 mile to the registration box at the trailhead and park under the tree.

The Ride

0.0 From the registration box, head away from the highway up the road.

0.4 Intersection; turn left and follow Mill Canyon Road. Right leads to Tusher Canyon (Rides 36 and 37) and Hidden Canyon (Ride 39). This spot is a good alternative trailhead.

1.0 Keep right. Left is where the Courthouse Rock option returns.

1.6 The Mill Canyon Dinosaur Trail (a footpath—no bikes please) is off to the right. It offers a fun diversion either now or at the end of the ride.

1.7 The trail becomes a grassy doubletrack that soon becomes sand. Small sand traps litter the path for the next 0.2 mile.

2.5 Spur roads go left; keep right to stay on the main road. The second spur, at the bottom of a wash by a cottonwood tree, is the entrance to the Courthouse Rock option (see below).

3.3 A brief stretch of rocks offers a technical respite from the sand.

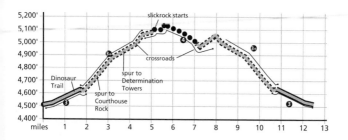

3.7   A spur goes right to Determination Towers. Stay left.

3.8   Another spur goes right to Determination Towers. Stay left.

4.1   Depending on recent weather, the dunes start here.

4.5   Mercifully, the tread returns to hardpack here.

4.6   Standing at the crossroads. Ahead to the left is the route—not the sharp left, but the second left. Look at the map if you have *any* doubt, since the wrong road could lead to the Abominable Sand Monster.

4.7   A road goes left. Stay right and continue up slickrock. Heading left is sandy and requires a right turn in 0.5 mile to get back on track.

5.5   The trail reaches a huge rock platform or flat spot that is shared by both buttes. This is the crossover point between the buttes. Pick your way clockwise around Monitor (on the left). When ready to cross over and head back, at around 6.1 miles, try to stay close to the butte to get the most out of the slickrock playground. *Please* avoid the cryptobiotic crust.

6.5   Back at the rock platform between the buttes, head around the backside (south) of Merrimac. Close to the butte is a good bet. The slickrock here offers endless possibilities! Enjoy, but beware of cliffs.

7.4   If you hit a road here, fine. Turn right onto it. If not you'll come to a fence on the rock. Follow the fence down and left to the road, then turn right. (Left is the return from the Determination Towers option and a sandy route to Utah Highway 313.)

7.9   Back at the crossroads (at mile 4.6 above). Turn left and retrace your route back to the trailhead. The Courthouse Rock option is a fun return for those with energy left.

Determination Towers Option: Ride this option on the way out. From mile 3.7 or 3.8, turn right (west) onto one of the two spurs. Go 0.4 mile, turn left, and ride up to the prominent towers. Go counterclockwise around the towers, and about three-quarters of the way around turn right onto a sandy road, keeping right of any spurs. In 1.1 miles it joins the main ride described above at mile 7.4. Left here leads to the crossroads (at mile 4.6 above) and the return leg to your car. Total mileage: 2.4 miles.

Courthouse Option: This option is good for the return trip. From mile 2.5 in the ride description (about mile 10.1 on the return ride), head east. This is a right turn on the return trip. In 0.1 mile stay left, following cairns to "A Rock with No Name." Avoid climbing immediately to the white slickrock, and wait for the ramp up about 1 mile into this route. Round the point and head north toward the trailhead. The road visible ahead is a good target. Take this road for 0.2 mile, then exit left onto slickrock. Keep working left to pick up the road that descends the wash on the left side. Keep left where the road joins in the wash, pass by the old stage stop, and rejoin the main trail at mile 1 in the description of the main ride. Total mileage: 3.1 miles.

36 Tusher Canyon's Left Side

Location: 17 miles north of Moab.

Distance: 8 8-mile minimum out-and-back from two-wheel-drive trailhead. Those with four-wheel-drive vehicles can subtract 4 miles by driving up the route and past the sand.

Approximate riding time: 2 hours plus play time.

Physical difficulty: Moderate. The sand saps even the strongest legs, so count on walking. The initial slickrock climb is on the steep side. But once on top, the terrain mellows out.

Technical difficulty: Moderate to challenging. The sand, if ridden, is a technical hassle. But the slickrock is awesome! It can be made technically easier or harder depending on your visual acuity and your route choice. In short, the line you choose should be your own.

Trail surface: 6.8 miles on gravel road; the rest (2.8 miles or more) is slickrock. The gravel road is very sandy for the last mile. The slickrock is expansive, sticky, orange, and pretty—some of the region's best.

Highlights: Looking for limitless slickrock fun? This is my favorite place to play! It takes some effort and attention to get on top of this rock, but once you do they may never get you to come down. Pack a lunch (and maybe the headphones with a tape of Ennio Morricone's *Fistful of Dollars*) and create fat-trax splendor. There's about a mile of sand to endure before reaching the canyon's rock, but this is avoidable with a four-wheeler.

Land status: BLM.

Map: USGS Jug Rock.

Finding the trailhead: From the intersection of Center and Main in Moab, drive 16.5 miles north on U.S. Highway 191. Turn left onto Mill Canyon Road, and cross the railroad tracks. It comes up rather quickly. Just look for the railroad to get really close to the road. Then, after mile marker 141, look for a MILL CANYON ROAD sign marking the

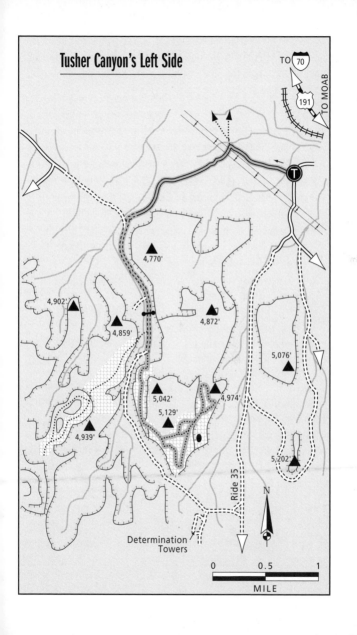

Tusher Canyon's Left Side

TO 70

TO MOAB

191

T

4,770'

4,902'

4,859'

4,872'

5,076'

5,042'

5,129'

4,974'

4,939'

5,202'

Ride 35

N

Determination
Towers

0   0.5   1

MILE

ramp up to the railroad tracks. Don't be fooled by the prominent No Trespassing sign. It pertains only to the railroad corridor. Follow this road 0.6 mile, past the Monitor and Merrimac trailhead, to a fork in the road. Park in the area provided.

The Ride

0.0 Take the right fork, signed TUSHER CANYON.

0.7 Stay left where the right fork follows the power lines.

2.1 Stay on the main road when it enters the sandy wash, then keep left and remain in the wash as the road goes right to Bartlett Wash and Hidden Canyon (Rides 38 and 39).

2.9 Keep left as a road leaves the wash to the right. Up to this point the wash is typically too sandy to ride well. Hope for damp, firm tread to begin here.

3.0 Fence. Close this gate behind you, and continue up the wash, which widens.

3.4 Ride up the long, obscure, eroded rock "ramp" that leaves the wash on the left at about a 30-degree angle. This grooved rock road heads up to the slickrock formation away from the demon sand!

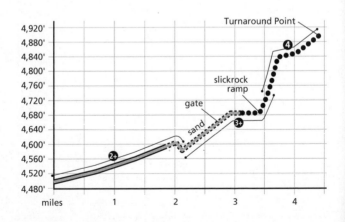

3.5 Look for a way up to the left of the rock knob, or plan on portaging up a rockslide. The gray rock below the slide rims out.

3.6 Weave through the rockslide. Dismount for the final 30 yards and lift your bike up the rock ledge. Cairns should help guide the way.

3.7 A geologic marker assures you of being on track after hopping up the ledge.

4.0 Look for a way up two rings of rock, and continue to advance, keeping as far left as possible as the route gets skinny.

4.3 Portage up one more layer as the trail gets pinched around the corner.

4.4 Another geological marker marks a good place to start looking for a route to the right of Tusher's Tiny Tower. If you pass on the left via the white rock, you'll need to hunt for an environmentally friendly way back to the red rock.

Route finding is now up to your own cerebellum. Before rushing off, look around and pick out something to use as a return landmark. Free-form fun awaits. Wander about a mile to the left to find a prehistoric half-pipe. But don't dive into its potholes or off the cliff at the end! When you're done, retrace the route home.

37 Tusher Too–Tusher Canyon's Right Side

Location: 15 miles north of Moab.

Distance: 9.8-mile out-and-back. A four-wheel-drive vehicle can get you farther in, reducing the ride to 4 miles.

Approximate riding time: 2 to 3 hours.

Physical difficulty: Moderate. The extremely sandy wash drains energy, and some of the slickrock is steep. Covering the early ground in a four-wheel-drive vehicle makes both Tusher rides much easier.

Technical difficulty: Moderate to challenging. The slickrock offers both easier and harder lines— moderate to challenging is the

average. The sand definitely adds to the initial difficulty.

Trail surface: 6.2 miles on four-wheel-drive road; 3.8 miles on slickrock. Actually, the slickrock measurement is the bare minimum. Exploration exponentially expands the slickrock factor.

Highlights: Not as expansive as Tusher's Left Side, this ride puts the same smooth stone beneath the rubber and its access is easier. Some exploration at the terminus of the ride is nice. But *please* don't do any more damage than has already occurred. If you can't find the crossover at mile 5.8, go back.

Land status: BLM.

Map: USGS Jug Rock.

Finding the trailhead: From the intersection of Center and Main in Moab, drive 16.5 miles north on U.S. Highway 191. Turn left onto Mill Canyon Road, and cross the railroad tracks. It comes up rather quickly; just look for the railroad to get really close to the road. Then, after mile marker 141, look for a sign that says MILL CANYON ROAD and marks the ramp up to the railroad tracks. Don't be fooled by the

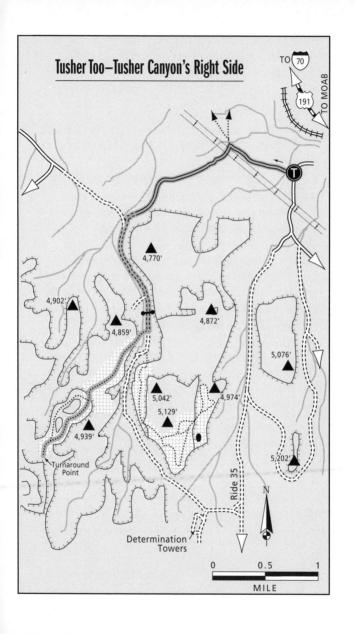

Tusher Too—Tusher Canyon's Right Side

TO 70

TO MOAB

191

T

4,770'

4,902'

4,859'

4,872'

5,076'

5,042'

5,129'

4,974'

4,939'

Turnaround
Point

5,202'

Ride 35

N

Determination
Towers

0   0.5   1

MILE

prominent No Trespassing sign. It pertains only to the railroad corridor. Follow this road 0.6 mile, past the Monitor and Merrimac trailhead, to a fork in the road. Park in the area provided.

The Ride

0.0 Head down the right-hand fork following the directions from Tusher's Left Side (Ride 36). Pick up this description at the fence at mile 3.0.

3.0 Fence. Pass through the gate and continue up the wash.

3.1 The wash widens and the road stays to the left side. Look for another wash to enter from the right. A small sandy trail takes off from here up to the rock formation that is Tusher's Right Side.

3.3 Stay on the sandy trail as it passes beneath a rock slide. Once on the rock, pick a line and go. A good rule-of-thumb is to keep the overhanging layer close at hand on the right.

3.8 A glance to the left reveals the Determination Towers through the gap off the end of Tusher's Left Side.

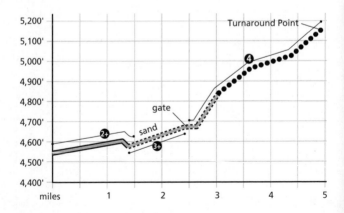

4.3 Time to turn right and head uphill; the lower layer is history. Lift over the 4-foot ledge, then ride straight up the rock if you can.

4.4 Turn left, and follow the route as it contours around the rock. Looking closely reveals a trail coming over from the other side of the ridge. This is the trail mentioned at mile 5.8.

4.8 The route once again pinches out. Head uphill to the top of the saddle.

4.9 The top of the saddle. From here you can turn around and retrace your tracks down the rock, pick a fresh line, or continue to the right around the other side of the ridge. Continuing around adds some portaging and requires extreme care to keep from damaging the environment. It's *not* recommended. If you do go, the crossover point is at mile 5.8 or so by a tiny wash that spills into the rock. A small cairn may mark the trail. If you can't find the route, *return*. Please don't make a new trail!

38 Bartlett Wash

Location: 18 miles north of Moab.

Distance: 6.1-mile loop or 4-mile out-and-back.

Approximate riding time: 1 hour minimum. Plan on a lot of play time on Bartlett's playground!

Physical difficulty: Moderate. Gradual lines up the rock are easy to find.

Technical difficulty: Moderate to challenging. How technical do you want it? The free-form nature of the ride allows route selection from moderate to challenging.

Trail surface: 2.8 miles on slickrock; 3.3 miles on four-wheel-drive road. This is primo rock candy! When ridden as a loop, count on some extremely sandy four-wheel-drive road. The amount of bikeable slickrock is limited only by the imagination and cliffs. The access road becomes gooey when wet, making access a four-wheel-drive affair.

Highlights: Rock and roll! For those who aren't compelled to stay within the lines, this may be the best slickrock riding around. The orange rock offers bowls and climbs as well as breathtaking cliffsides. Photographers, bring your cameras! Magazine quality photos are found here—orange rock with a deep blue-sky background. Voila!

Land status: BLM.

Map: USGS Jug Rock.

Finding the trailhead: From Center Street in Moab, drive 18 miles north on U.S. Highway 191. Turn left onto Blue Hills Road and go 2.4 miles, then turn left onto a dirt spur. Drive 0.8 mile to a fork in the road. Right leads up to the alternate parking for those following the loop option. All others go straight at the fork, and drive 0.5 mile to an extremely sandy wash across the road. Scout it first to decide whether your vehicle can cross it. Those parking here should pull to the side and follow the access directions to the trailhead. Otherwise, continue up the hill, turn right, and stay right. About 0.5 from the wash is a wooded glade. Enter it via the faint left at the top of a hill.

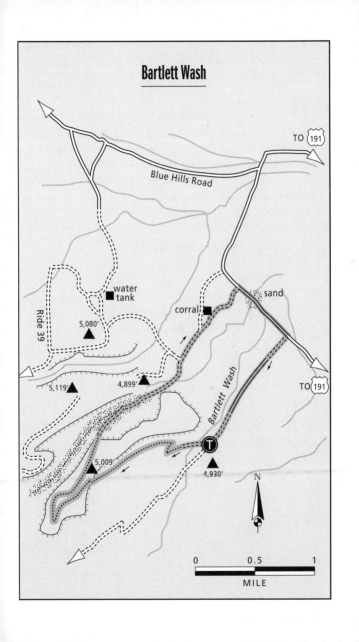

Bartlett Wash

TO (191)

Blue Hills Road

water
tank

sand

corral

Ride 39

5,080'

5,119'   4,899'

Bartlett Wash

TO (191)

5,009'

T

N

4,930'

0   0.5   1

MILE

This makes a nice parking area. From the glade, pedal up the wash. Since a variety of parking spots are available, the odometer readings start at the fence about 0.7 mile up the wash.

The Ride

0.0 Pass through the fence after dancing in and out of the wash. Forty yards ahead is an unmarked trail on the right. Follow it over to the slickrock. Climb up onto the rock, and head up and left. Stay on the flat rock, continuing to head left.

0.2 Hop up the ledge's low point and switchback to gain some elevation. Then quickly turn back to the left, and continue following the rock strata.

0.5 Cross the sand to the next rock section.

0.6 At the next rock stay low on the lighter-colored layer. It's free-form from here.

1.9 If you went straight for the tip of the rock, this mileage is close. It continues to be rideable around this point to the other side of the canyon. I recommend playing around, then finding a route back the way you came to get maximum

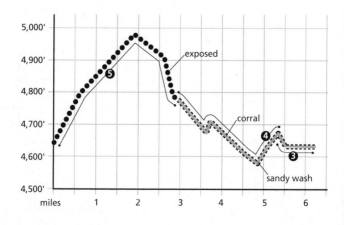

slickrock pleasure. But for those who must ride in loops, the description continues.

2.6 A couple of hairy, exposed sidehills are necessary to clean the descent to the valley. Portage your bike, carefully.

2.8 Drop onto the valley floor at this insanely sandy road. It weaves in and out of the wash without any real relief from the sand.

3.7 Finally the sand gives way to a packed-sediment descent and rocky climb. The going is much better from now on.

4.1 Stay right past the spurs, arriving at a corral. Turn right here, and descend to the main access road. Left heads to the same road but farther from the car. This corral makes a good alternate trailhead.

4.5 Turn right at this T intersection and find the car. This is the road in the access directions. Follow it across the wash and up the hill. Turn right at the top of the hill.

6.1 Loop complete. Keep in mind, mileages are without any slickrock playing. Yours will probably be higher.

39 Hidden Canyon North

Location: 20 miles north of Moab.

Distance: 7.4-mile minimum out-and-back. Plenty of play areas can add distance.

Approximate riding time: 1 to 2 hours allows only minimal play time.

Physical difficulty: Moderate. Many novices will find this aerobically acceptable.

Technical difficulty: Moderate to challenging. The roads to the play areas are moderate, while the slickrock can be challenging, depending upon the chosen path.

Trail surface: 6.8 miles on four-wheel-drive road; it's up to you on the slickrock. The four-wheel-drive road is initially eroded dirt. The latter parts of the ride are very sandy. The slickrock offers expansive playgrounds of white sandstone. The access road becomes gooey when wet, making this a four-wheel-drive affair.

Highlights: Hidden Canyon is one of those sights that stops all action except jaw gaping. Only nature could craft something so perfectly chaotic. Parallel rings of color, barely tilted, rise above the sand and brush floor. Each seemingly insignificant groove helps continue the sculpting of this treasure. Leading to the canyon, blankets of wrinkled white sandstone provide three expansive play areas, the third bordered by a wire-thin canyon. The actual Hidden Canyon bursts suddenly upon riders who pedal onward after crossing the wire canyon's head on a sandy road. This area has seen a lot of abuse. Hopefully these directions will help people enjoy the area without destroying the fragile soils around it. Read the section on cryptobiotic crust in the Introduction before setting out on this ride.

Land status: BLM.

Map: USGS Jug Rock.

Finding the trailhead: From Moab drive 18 miles north on U.S. Highway 191 to Blue Hills Road, and turn left. Keep right at mile 2.4,

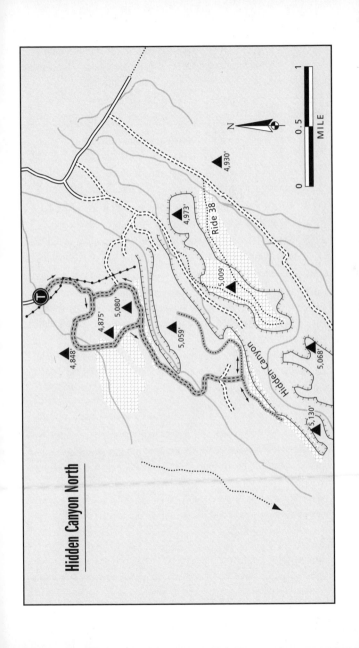

Hidden Canyon North

4,848'
4,875'
5,080'
5,059'
4,973'
5,009'
5,068'
5,130'
4,930'

Ride 38

Hidden Canyon

N

MILE

0   0.5   1

passing the road to Bartlett Wash, and turn left at mile 3.7 onto a dirt spur. Stay left at mile 4.0 where another road joins. After crossing a wash at mile 4.4, look for a parking area on the right.

The Ride

0.0 Take a right from the parking area, and pedal south on the road.

0.3 Keep right and pass through a fence. This is an alternate parking spot and the beginning of the ride's longest climb.

0.6 Pass a water tank and stay right. The road to the left is the return route.

0.8 Stay left through this zone. The road is packed dirt with rocks and some sand.

1.1 Keep left here.

1.2 Enter the first slickrock playground. It's the right or northern-most slickrock of the two formations that have been visible. When playing here avoid areas of soil! *Please stay off the cryptobiotic crust.*

1.4 The exit from this play area is 0.2 mile from the entrance on the left edge of the rock. A cairn marks the crossover point

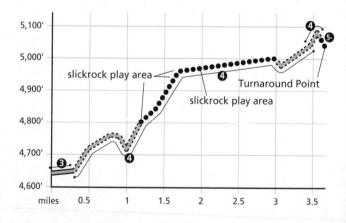

to the next playground. It's best to find this spot before exploring the slickrock too far. Return here when ready to crossover and stop on the ridge. From here you can see how to exit across the rock. It's about 0.2 mile straight across to the steep, eroded road that continues the ride. (Remember: These odometer readings don't count exploratory miles.)

1.7 After the second playground, the exit crosses over a low ridge and into another slickrock zone joining another four-wheel-drive road. The road runs west and south for 1.4 miles, then crosses over a wash (at mile 3.1) and heads to the payoff of the ride. Advanced riders will enjoy some fabulous terrain left of this road while heading for the crossover point. Play "keep off the crust" and have fun.

3.1 This is the crossover point. Turn left onto the sandy double-track.

3.5 Stay straight at this three-way intersection.

3.7 Wow! Gawk at Hidden Canyon. Wipe your chin before heading out onto this exposed rock. Use good crust ethics and mind the edges. Don't try to get to the bottom—the only route involves rock climbing. Besides, the bottom is too sandy to be enjoyable. Retrace the route back to the crossover at mile 1.7. Then stay right and continue down the road. Roll another 1.1 miles to the trailhead.

40 Gold Bar Rim

Location: 10 miles north of Moab.

Distance: 12.2-mile one-way to the Portal Trail, then 2.5 miles more to Potash Road or 17.4-mile out-and-back.

Approximate riding time: 2.5 to 3 hours.

Physical difficulty: Strenuous. The slickrock bed that underlies this route is severely tilted, causing extreme physical strain for Homo *veloterra* specimens who attempt to reach the formation's rim. Translation: This ride to the sky be steep.

Technical difficulty: Challenging. The ride starts out technically serene (moderate) and gets increasingly more challenging as it ascends the aforementioned slope. Want more challenge? Tack on the Portal Trail. Insane!

Trail surface: 4.7 miles on gravel road; 7.5 miles on four-wheel-drive road. This bad boy starts off on a packed dirt road, heads through some eroded spots, then finishes off with killer slickrock. It is a four-wheel-drive road in name only. The scrapes and an occasional grease stain are the only differences between a normal rock trail and the "jeep" route.

Highlights: The views are great. But this trail's serpentine route over a huge, eroded slab of white slickrock is the main draw. As an out-and-back ride to the rim it's fun. As a shuttle route with the Portal Trail added on it becomes epic. Another option is to hook into the Poison Spider Mesa Trail (see Ride 31). The trail's gentle start allows legs to limber up and often draws peak performances from riders. A ride worth its weight in memories.

Land status: BLM.

Maps: USGS Merrimac Butte, Gold Bar Rim, Moab.

Finding the trailhead: From Center and Main in Moab, drive 9.9 miles north on U.S. Highway 191. Turn left into the trailhead parking area, which is easily visible from the road. If you reach Utah Highway 313, you've gone too far. This is also the end point of the Gemini Bridges route (Ride 33).

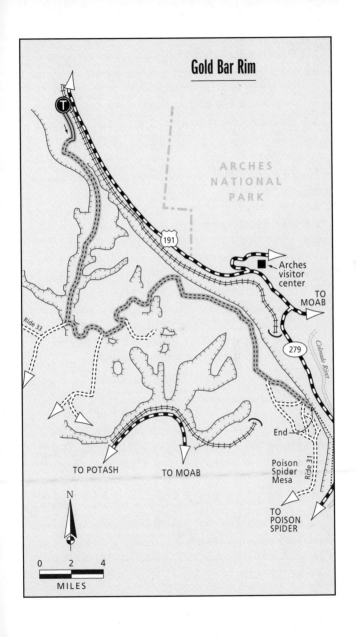

Gold Bar Rim

ARCHES
NATIONAL
PARK

191

Arches
visitor
center

TO
MOAB

279

Colorado River

Ride 33

Ride 31

End

Poison
Spider
Mesa

TO POTASH

TO MOAB

TO
POISON
SPIDER

N

0   2   4

MILES

The Ride

0.0 From the parking area, head away from the highway, across the railroad tracks, and immediately left onto the gravel road. It's intermittently washboarded and eroded.

2.8 Stay on the main road up the hill and past the spurs. The road descends and levels out through a wide, rock-walled canyon.

4.9 Keep left at this fork. Right heads up to Gemini Bridges.

5.2 Turn left here.

6.0 One more left.

6.9 Keep right at this faint fork.

8.1 This point delivers vistas of the La Sal Mountains ahead and the twisted terrain of Bull Canyon and Day Canyon behind.

8.3 Stay left, and look for "jeep skat" (scrapes and oil and tire marks) that marks the way. Cairns also assist in navigation.

8.7 First overlook. Out-and-backers should turn around here. If continuing to the Portal Trail, follow the cairns. This requires keen, attentive eyes. The trail loses a lot of altitude, then heads up and down as it romps along the rim.

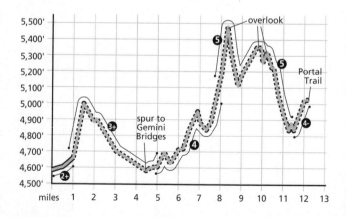

11.3 Don't miss this critical left turn out of the wash. Some people keep riding right on down the wash. But it's not a hard turn to see. The road drops into the wash for about 5 yards and climbs up the other side for the final grind to The Portal.

12.2 The Portal Trail heads straight away and the Poison Spider route (Ride 31) follows the road on the right.

41 White Rim

Location: 30 miles west of Moab in the Island In The Sky District of Canyonlands National Park.
Distance: 103.1-mile loop.
Approximate riding time: 10 hours plus a nap and meals for the superhuman, or a three- to five-day sag-supported (four-wheel-drive required) expedition for mortals. The ride described here goes clockwise around the loop in four days and three nights.
Physical difficulty: Moderate. To attempt this 103.1-mile loop as a day ride borders on psychotic—but who said you have to be sane to ride a mountain bike? Ridden over four days, however, it ranks as moderate, with one major (strenuous!) climb scheduled for each day. Day one consists of a huge descent, then easy grades. Day two adds some climbing near White Crack and then a frightfully steep wall innocently named Murphy's Hogback. More descending starts day three for some great unwinding, but, to keep riders honest, Hardscrabble is a day's worth of climbing in one shot. The final day sees a long sandy spin along the Green River and an inhuman climb up Horsethief Trail. This is followed by a long gradual grind that is easily avoided with a shuttle.

Technical difficulty: Moderate. A few slickrock patches, bedrock drops, and eroded ruts keep things interesting. But these obstacles are small and widely spread out. The fast and furious drop down the Shafer Trail has savage grades and harrowing hairpins. The rest of the day's spin is mild, with some ledges near camp. The road to White Crack, on day two, includes a steep, sandy hill that is very tough to clean. Murphy's Hogback is so steep that the gradient is the main obstacle. Bar ends, low gearing, and energy are required! Day three has by far the most technical riding—slickrock and ledges show up frequently. Hardscrabble Bottom offers differing challenges depending upon the conditions. The last day has a sandy theme. Seasoned sand riders will enjoy the riverside stroll while the rest grit their teeth and enjoy the scenery anyway. Horsethief Trail is steep but rates a moderate technically, as do the washboards back to the visitor center.

Trail surface: 78.8 miles on four-wheel-drive road; 12.6 miles on gravel road; 11.7 miles on paved road (which is avoidable with a shuttle). The four-wheel-drive road is mostly packed dirt and in pretty good shape. Some sections feature slickrock, ledges, clay, and sand. After Murphy's Hogback the road delivers more technical intricacies for the next 12 miles. Hardscrabble Bottom can be very soft if recently graded (yes, graded), extremely muddy and goopy if wet, and very rough if it has been wet, used, then dried and not yet graded. Actually the whole trail changes character when wet and may require chains for the sag vehicle! The Shafer and Horsethief Trails can be closed in wet weather.

Highlights: The White Rim is famous as the ultimate canyon country ride. Though more and more people ride this in one day, they're missing the point. This trail is about being with friends in one of the most scenic regions in the world.

Do this ride clockwise with a four-wheel-drive sag vehicle. Aiming for Gooseberry, Murphy, and Hardscrabble Campgrounds makes for a good, moderate ride with one aerobic assault daily. Spring and fall are the prime times to make this epic journey.

▶ When thinking of these rocks one must not conceive of piles of boulders or heaps of fragments, but of a whole land of naked rock, with giant forms carved on it: cathedral-shaped buttes, towering hundreds or thousands of feet, cliffs that cannot be scaled, and canyon walls that shrink the river into insignificance, with vast, hollow domes and tall pinnacles and shafts set on the verge overhead; and all highly colored—buff, gray, red, brown, and chocolate—never lichened, never moss-covered, but bare, and often polished.

—John Wesley Powell

Don't even think of riding this during summer. It's just too hot and is probably unsafe. No-see-ums usually become a problem in late May and stick around into summer. Riding clockwise puts the Green River at the end of the trip, a possible emergency water source from Queen Anne's Bottom to Mineral Bottom (purify all water). If time and supplies allow, camp in the Island in the Sky Campground the night before the journey. Also be sure you're stocked up on water before leaving town. The park doesn't have any water for visitors. Plan on at *least* a gallon a day per rider plus water for creature comforts. Low-impact campers will be happy they learned about the dishwashing properties of sand.

Land status: Canyonlands National Park, Island in the Sky District. *Permits are required for overnight use.* And they're not easily obtained. Permit requests must be mailed to National Park Service Reservation Office, 2282 South West Resource Boulevard, Moab, UT 84532-3298; Fax: (435) 259-4285; www.nps.gov/cany/reserve.htm. A $30 nonrefundable fee must accompany the request. Checks, money order, VISA, or MasterCard are accepted by mail (use a credit card when faxing). Make checks payable to the National Park Service. Each request must have the trip leader's name, address, and daytime phone number; the number of vehicles and people in the trip; dates and campsites requested; and the money. It is highly recommended to include at least one set of alternate dates and/or campsites. Allow at least six months lead time. Pick up permits at the park visitor center. Carefully read all of the Park Service literature to be fully prepared. Regulations change; know and obey them. Reservations can be made starting on the second Monday in July for the next calendar year. The maximum group size is fifteen people with three vehicles.

Reservation help is available by phone Monday through Friday from 8:00 A.M. to 12:30 P.M. (Mountain time) at (435) 259-4351 or via e-mail (canyres@nps.gov).

Maps: USGS Musselman Arch, Monument Basin, Turks Head, Upheaval Dome, Horsethief Canyon, Bowknot Bend, Mineral Canyon, The Knoll.

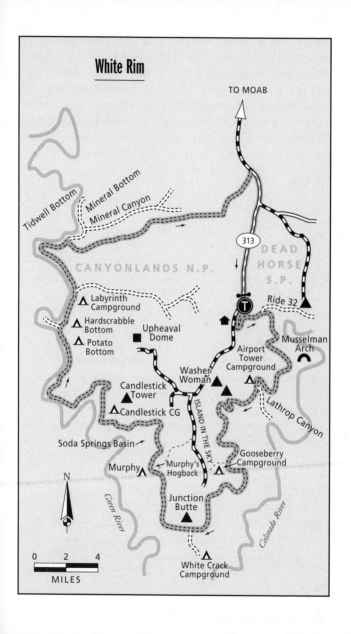

White Rim

TO MOAB

Tidwell Bottom

Mineral Bottom

Mineral Canyon

(313)

DEAD HORSE S.P.

CANYONLANDS N.P.

Ride 32

Labyrinth Campground

Hardscrabble Bottom

Potato Bottom

Upheaval Dome

Musselman Arch

Airport Tower Campground

Lathrop Canyon

Washer Woman

Candlestick Tower

Candlestick CG

ISLAND IN THE SKY

Soda Springs Basin

Gooseberry Campground

Murphy

Murphy's Hogback

N

Green River

Junction Butte

Colorado River

0   2   4

MILES

White Crack Campground

Finding the trailhead: From Center and Main in Moab, drive 11 miles north on U.S. Highway 191 to Utah Highway 313. Turn left and stay on the road all the way to the park gate. Continue about 0.5 mile past the visitor center to a parking area on the left. To avoid pedaling a long, washboarded stretch on the final day, leave a shuttle vehicle where Horsethief Trail tops out from Mineral Bottom. Drive 12.6 miles west on the access road that leaves from the west side of Utah 313 about 8.9 miles north of the visitor center.

The Ride

0.0 From the parking area, turn right and pedal north toward the visitor center.

0.5 Visitor center. Be sure you've picked up your permit. Continue down the main road toward the park entrance gate.

1.5 Turn right onto the Shafer Trail. It's the dirt road on the right before you reach the park gate.

3.3 Brake check! The road drops away as it plunges toward the Colorado River.

6.8 The road forks. Keep right on the official White Rim Road. Left goes to the Shafer Campsite and then to Potash Road.

8.1 The Goose Neck Trail (no bikes) goes left for an up close and personal view of its namesake and the Colorado River. It's a 0.7-mile round-trip hike.

9.8 The Walking Rocks Trail walks off to the left. This foot trail is a 0.4-mile round-trip.

10.0 Musselman Arch. Take pictures and walk the arch if you dare, but *do not* take your bike off the road or on the arch!

16.0 The top of a brief climb that separates the drainage of Little Bridge Canyon (behind) and Lathrop Canyon (ahead).

17.9 Lathrop Canyon foot trail leaves to the right en route to Island in the Sky. In 0.1 mile the day-use-only Lathrop Canyon Road leaves to the left and drops almost 500 feet in 3.5 miles down to the Colorado River.

18.8 Airport Tower campsites start here on the right. That big hunk of rock watching over this wide plateau is Airport Tower.

20.1 Washer Woman Rock slaves under the oppressive glare of Monster Tower where the road skirts the North Fork of Buck Canyon. The road then rounds Buck to continue past the Middle Fork and finally the South Fork at mile 27.

29.4 Gooseberry Trail heads up to Island in the Sky as the road rounds the point of Gooseberry Canyon. Campsites A and B lie just ahead on the left.

32.7 The pulloff area for viewing Monument Basin comes up just after this rise. This is yet another wipe-off-the-chin view. There are more views into the basin through mile 36. Can you pick out the Totem Pole?

33.6 The road appears to fork, but tracks that lead down the wash on the right are from lost bikers. Do not follow them; keep left.

37.5 The road forks after this rise. The left-hand road leads 1.5 miles to White Crack Campsite on the point of the White Rim, a place worth visiting. One prohibitively sandy hill forces

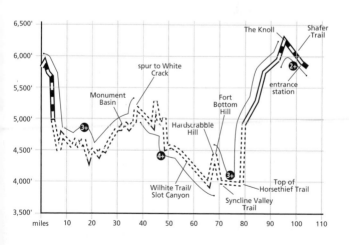

most riders to walk. White Crack has archaeological artifacts spread throughout the site. *Please leave them undisturbed.* Allow others to experience the same thrill of finding them (and preserve the site for further archaeological study). This is a nice campsite if you can secure it. To continue the main loop, go right at the fork, pedaling past Junction Butte above and on the right.

44.0 Time to pay for all the downhill. Cross the wash, and start up the first pitch of Murphy's Hogback. This is only a warm-up for the final assault at mile 44.7. The southern branch of the Hogback trail leaves here for Island in the Sky.

45.1 The top of Murphy's Hogback delivers views of the entire planet and has three campsites. A rim-side seat from camp C gives vistas of Candlestick Tower (north-northwest), '50-Chevy Rock (north), and Soda Springs Basin (northwest). The north branch of the Hogback trail leaves from up here.

55.6 Candlestick Campsite. This camp works well on a four-night trip using Airport Towers, White Crack, Candlestick, and Labyrinth or Taylor Campsites.

57.9 After the most technical portion of trail so far, the Wilhite Trail heads right and up toward the Island. The wash crosses the road and enters a slot canyon. Confident friction climbers can dismount and follow it down to see its beauty from within. Farther down the road, the Green River's Valentine Bottom comes into view.

62.1 An emergency water road leads down to Queen Anne's Bottom to the left. Keep bombing down the main road, and you won't even see it.

63.1 The road turns right, leaving lovely Queen Anne's Bottom behind and bearing toward Beaver Bottom. (I'm not making these names up, but apparently some lonely prospector did!)

66.0 The first of three Potato Bottom campsites. The next two are 0.6 and 0.7 mile farther, but all are in Potato Bottom Basin. *Warning:* Hardscrabble Hill lies dead ahead.

67.0 Up, up, and away. Hardscrabble Hill is here. Where's that 20-tooth front chainring when you need it?

68.2 Top. Don't go flying down the hill if you want to visit the ruins described at mile 68.6.

68.6 The road to the Fort Bottom trail goes left just after this corner. The road goes 0.5 mile to the foot trail, which leads another 1.2 miles to a ruin, thought to be Fremont, and an old cabin. The ruined tower is thought to be either defensive or ceremonial in purpose. The cabin was to be a stopping place for tuberculosis patients on their way to a never-built refuge near the confluence of the Colorado and Green Rivers.

70.3 The road turns right. Hardscrabble campsites are to the left.

71.6 The Syncline Valley foot trail through Upheaval Canyon to the Upheaval Dome goes right.

72.3 Keep left as the four-wheel-drive road to Taylor Campsite and Zeus and Moses Tower leaves to the right.

72.4 Labyrinth Campsite. The road ahead continues to be sandy and is now narrow. Sag drivers beware.

78.7 Turn right and head up to Horsethief Trail, which gains a gargantuan hunk of altitude in 1.5 miles. Left heads to Mineral Bottom.

80.2 Top. Look down on what you've accomplished!

80.3 This is where your shuttle vehicle should be parked. Otherwise ride this washboarded road back to the trailhead, avoiding all spurs.

92.9 Turn right on the paved road and follow it back to the park.

101.6 Visitor center.

103.1 Parking lot and trailhead. Hug your companions and revel in the conclusion of an odyssey while mourning its passing.

42 The Kokopelli Trail

Location: From Loma, Colorado, to Moab.

Distance: 140.4-mile one-way. Or riders can take their pick among six sections: Section 1 is 20.4 miles; 2 is 33 miles; 3 is 20.6 miles; 4 is 17.8 miles; 5 is 24.2 miles; and 6 is 24.4 miles. The sections outlined below are logistically sensible, but strong riders may want to combine sections for longer days.

Approximate riding time: Six days with shuttle vehicles. Ordinary cars are sufficient for all but Section 4, which requires a four-wheel-drive or described route adaptations to accommodate cars.

Physical difficulty: Strenuous. Ridden end to end, Kokopelli is long and the steeps are littered throughout. Section 1 is moderate except for the strenuous steep out of Salt Creek. Section 2 is moderate except for the steep out of Bitter Creek. Section 3 is moderate except for the obscenely strenuous 4 miles of sand. Section 4 is strenuous, with lots of climbing! Section 5 goes back to moderate. Hammerheads can add this section to Section 4 or 6 to shorten the overall ride by one day. Section 6 is strenuous, but the climb is on pavement and it's all downhill from the midpoint.

Technical difficulty: Moderate to challenging. While there's plenty of spinning, the obstacles are numerous and diverse. And remote. Section 1 is moderate to challenging with goodly amounts of singletrack and slickrock challenges. Section 2 is also moderate to challenging, pretty straightforward with some tough spots. Section 3 is moderate or challenging depending on whether you try to ride cleanly through the sand. The rest of the section is moderate. Section 4 is moderate to challenging, but the Cottonwood Canyons are rugged. Section 5 is moderate, and once on the gravel road things get easy. Section 6 is moderate to challenging; after dropping off the Loop Road, watch for erosion ruts in the fast, downhill four-wheel-drive section. Just before joining Sand Flats Road, the ruts are particularly deep and nasty. The obstacles may seem easier than they should be. Probably because all cylinders are firing when riding the Kokopelli! A few ledges on the drop to the Porcupine Rim stock tanks finish off the difficult terrain unless you opt to ride the Slickrock Trail before hitting Moab.

Trail surface: 140.4 miles on every type of surface imaginable. Section 1, Loma to Rabbit Valley, gets down to business with packed dirt, powdered red fluff, slickrock, sand, creek crossings, and craggy rock. Section 2 continues to the Cisco boat launch. The rugged four-wheel-drive roads on this route are eroded in places, and drainage crossings and slickrock sections are fun challenges. Section 3 leads riders to the Dewey Bridge on good packed surfaces. Pavement begins at mile 11.0, a major decision point. From here the main trail runs rough, then extremely sandy. The scenery is great, but the sand is as fun as a trip to an oral surgeon. Some riders opt to follow Utah Highway 128 to Dewey Bridge. Section 4, from the bridge to Onion Creek,

offers good packed-gravel road. As the Dolores Overlook route (Ride 6) peels off, the Kokopelli becomes extremely rough again throughout the second Cottonwood Canyon and into Fisher Valley, where it joins Onion Creek (Ride 7) and meets Section 5. From Forest Road 033 in Section 5, the road follows 2.6 miles of loose gravel, then 5.4 miles of pavement to the intersection of Gateway Road and the La Sal Loop Road. Section 6, the homestretch, drops onto a moderately rough four-wheel-drive road, then follows Sand Flats Road, which is initially eroded and rough but becomes graded from the Porcupine Rim trailhead down into Moab.

Highlights: Come on, this is the Kokopelli Trail! This is an adventure to tell the grandkids about. It is easier to supply than the White Rim Trail, but it's also tougher both technically and physically. Don't ride this on a whim. Permits aren't needed, but good planning is. The desert doesn't mess around, so bring too much water and make sure your shuttle vehicle carries extra potable gallons as well. The ride breaks down into six days, each with its own flavor. Day one tests riders' legs and power in Colorado country and straining up the Salt Creek steep. Day two has been revamped courtesy of the railroad and BLM, weaving among the Bitter Creek and Coal Draw drainages. Day three is all in Utah and is pleasant until it gets extremely sandy, but even this is incredibly scenic. Day four sends riders up a long hill with numerous spur options and slickrock play areas. Day five gives a day in the saddle to get out the kinks and do some fast road descending. Some riders may want to tack on the long grind of a climb on Section 6 and camp at Cold Springs. The final day climbs up to the majestic mountain site of Mason Draw, then runs along the beginning of Porcupine Rim (the rim, not the ride) to skirt Rill Creek Canyon. The route then rolls leisurely along Sand Flats before the sudden drop into Moab. Campsites along the way provide self-supported bikers a place to spread out.

Land status: Manti-La Sal National Forest, BLM Moab and Grand Junction Districts, and private holdings.

Maps: USGS Mack, Ruby Canyon, Bitter Creek Well, Westwater, Agate, Big Triangle, Cisco, Dewey, Blue Chief Mesa, Fisher Valley, Mount Waas, Warner Lake, Rill Creek, Moab. That's $56 worth of maps! The Grand Junction, Westwater, and Moab maps in the 1:100,000 series cover the route in a smaller scale and still show campsites.

Finding the trailhead: The start of each section is the end of the previous section. Shuttle/support cars should be placed at both access points. To access the Westwater Ranger Station in Section 2, use exit 225 on Interstate 70.

Loma: Section 1—From Moab take Utah 128 to I-70 East. Exit I-70 at Loma, exit 15. At the intersection on the south side of I-70, take the road eastward away from the Port of Entry station. The road heads down to a boat ramp. This is the start of The Kokopelli Trail.

Rabbit Valley: Section 2—Exit I-70 at Rabbit Valley, exit 2, and head south. Look for the parking area, a wide place in the road, in just

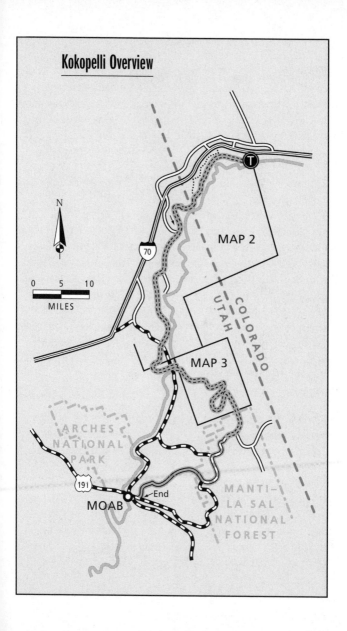

Kokopelli Overview

N

0 5 10
MILES

70

MAP 2

UTAH
COLORADO

MAP 3

T

ARCHES
NATIONAL
PARK

191

MOAB

End

MANTI–
LA SAL
NATIONAL
FOREST

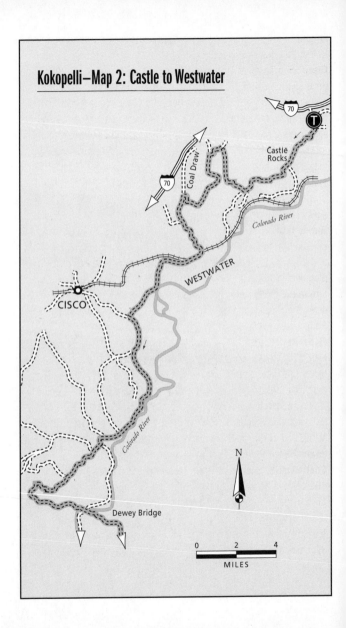

Kokopelli—Map 2: Castle to Westwater

70

T

Castle
Rocks

Coal Draw

70

Colorado River

WESTWATER

CISCO

Colorado River

N

Dewey Bridge

0   2   4
MILES

under 0.3 mile. The trail enters a bit farther down the road and turns to join this road and start Section 2.

Cisco Boat Launch: Section 3—From I-70 take Cisco exit 202, and drive south on Utah 128. When the highway turns right to Moab, continue straight toward Cisco. Just before "town" turn right onto Pumphouse Road. In 2.9 miles you'll come across the sign that says CISCO BOAT LANDING; FISH FORD. Follow the sign toward the Cisco Boat Launch. After 0.9 mile the road crosses a bridge, then forks. Keep left, no longer following the boat launch signs (it's to the right). Park in the area provided west of the cattleguard. From Moab drive north on Utah 128 to the above intersection and turn right. Exit 212 offers a gravel route into Cisco.

Dewey Bridge: Section 4— From Center and Main in Moab, drive 2.6 miles north on U.S. Highway 191. Turn right onto Utah Highway 128, and drive 30.8 miles northeast to the Dewey recreation site, complete with outhouses. Go another 0.2 mile, and look for a right-hand turn in the middle of a curve. It's easy to miss as you prepare to cross the Colorado River. Turn right here, and park by the old Dewey Bridge.

Fisher Valley: Section 5—This requires a four-wheel-drive sag wagon. Turn right onto Onion Creek Road up from Utah 128, 23.6 miles from Moab (22 miles from the turnoff of U.S. Highway 191). Drive up the rough, wet road 10 miles to the 16.2-mile point of Onion Creek (Ride 7). Those with low-clearance cars can either park at the Polar Mesa trailhead (Ride 8), at the turn at mile 4.3 of the Polar Mesa Trail, or at the end of the Onion Creek Trail. This last option adds a wet-n-wild downhill (see Ride 7).

Castle Valley: Section 6—From Moab drive 2.6 miles north on US 191 to Utah 128. Turn right, passing Matrimony Spring, and continue 16.1 miles. Turn right onto Castleton Road, and follow it to the intersection with the Loop Road.

Moab: Park at the visitor center, your hotel/campground, or at the Slickrock trailhead. There is no overnight parking at the visitor center!

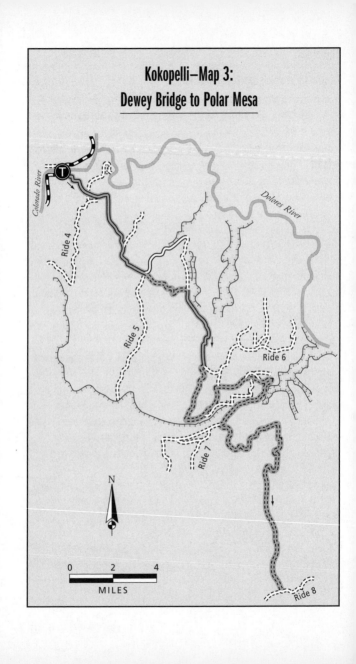

Kokopelli–Map 3:
Dewey Bridge to Polar Mesa

Colorado River

Dolores River

Ride 4

Ride 5

Ride 6

Ride 7

Ride 8

N

0   2   4
MILES

The Ride

Loma to Rabbit Valley—Section 1

0.0 From the parking area, pedal back toward I-70 on the access road. At the intersection turn left onto the gravel road.

1.3 The road forks. Keep left and head up the switchback.

1.6 Another fork; stay right.

2.8 Again, stay right. Some rim riding lies down the trail!

3.1 Keep right at yet another fork.

4.0 Pick up the cairns and BLM markers as the singletrack starts.

4.2 Gate. The trail continues on the other side. Gettin' techy!

6.0 Keep left here. It should be marked! If you're on a gravel road that's awfully sandy, you missed the main route and are heading to I-70. The singletrack is also sandy, but it's an actual trail. Continue to follow the markers and cairns.

10.3 Cross the slickrock. Again, cairns should blaze the way.

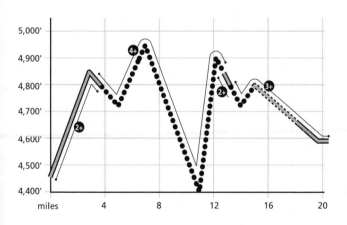

11.8   Use the footbridge to cross Salt Creek. This is a recent trail addition to keep bikers from being swept downstream. Followed by a monster hill.

13.5   Top! Enjoy the view while sucking in some air.

13.7   Turn right onto the gravel road.

15.7   Turn left at this intersection. Keep on this main road through any and all spurs.

19.7   Keep right here. A friendly Kokopelli marker should point the way.

20.2   Follow the right fork after this cattleguard.

20.4   Turn left at a T intersection. Section 2 begins here.

Rabbit Valley to Cisco—Section 2

0.0   Continue down the gravel road, going left from mile 20.4 of Section 1.

0.2   The road forks. Keep right, and thank the powers that be for granting access.

0.6   Another fork. Go left and cross the wash.

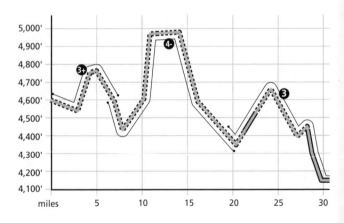

1.0 Again with the forks! Keep left, follow the road down through McDonald Creek Canyon, and stay left as a road joins.

2.0 Stay left on the main road.

3.1 Turn right at this fork. This area is particularly well blazed.

7.1 Turn right and descend toward Bitter Creek.

8.1 Keep right, except to pass, as the road follows the west side of Bitter Creek.

9.9 Again, keep right. Markers should still help to ease your mind.

10.5 Hang a Louie—that's a left turn—and start up the main hill of this section.

11.3 Cruise along the mesa top by keeping right here.

16.5 Turn left on the gravel road toward Westwater. You may actually see someone on this road.

20.4 Keep right as the old Kokopelli route enters, then go under the bridge. Turn right again where the road crosses the creek. Luckily, this is also well marked.

21.8 Keep left and go left again in 0.1 mile.

23.1 Cairns point the way out of the wash and over the slickrock.

25.6 Stay on the main road through three intersections here.

27.2 Keep left around this bend. A spur leaves to the right. Crank it out on the big ring while staying on the main road.

29.5 Keep left as several roads join the party from the right.

33.0 Turn right and head to the Cisco Boat Launch, just ahead, which marks the end of Section 2.

Cisco to Dewey Bridge—Section 3

0.0 Head back toward Cisco, going left with your back to the river.

1.7 Turn left toward the Cisco Fish Ford.

3.0 A marked but otherwise indiscernible trail splits right as the road makes a gradual bend left. There is also a spring nearby. Just keep an eye peeled for the marker on the right and follow it.

6.3 Cairns mark the way over this slickrock.

6.9 Keep right here following the river. The trail jumps up and continues to follow the river.

8.2 Gate. Follow the road on the other side as it drops toward Utah 128.

9.3 Keep right, and continue to crank to the highway.

11.0 Utah 128. Watch for traffic and turn left.

11.2 Decision time! After passing some corrals, the main route leaves the highway. The trail surface becomes extremely sandy. (Where's a camel when you need one?) But the scenery is pretty. Riders who want to avoid the sand can continue on Utah 128 to Dewey Bridge. Otherwise, turn right here and don't say I didn't warn you.

11.7 Continue to slug it up the road as another road enters on the right.

13.4 The road forks; keep left and roll down past the gate.

14.4 Keep right and enjoy the lack of deep sand.

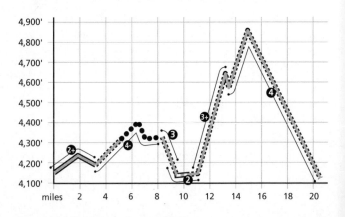

14.7 Watch for trail markers leading to a left turn.

15.2 Keep following the signs. One points right. What? No more difficult sand?

15.5 Left turn. Hop down the ledges, and follow the dotted lines across the slickrock. Enjoy this playground and the free-rolling tread. More sand awaits.

16.1 Intersection; keep left. Has it gotten sandier?

16.3 Another intersection. Stay right.

16.6 Praise the BLM and the signs, and turn left. Yes, it might be getting sandy soon.

18.5 One more left here.

19.5 Continue to follow the markers to and around the gravel pit.

20.6 Cross Utah 128, turn left to the abandoned gas station, and then turn right to cross Dewey Bridge. The sign at the start of Section 4 gives the dope on the bridge.

Dewey Bridge to Onion Creek—Section 4

0.0 This section begins by following the Top of the World route (see Ride 5). Head southeast up the gravel road, away from

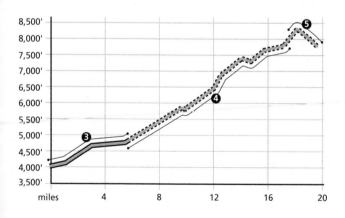

Dewey Bridge. Avoid all spurs for 5.1 miles. The road rolls up and down before settling into a constant climb.

3.4 The road passes a couple of slickrock playgrounds, then Cowskin Campground comes up on the left. The road turns right and grows steeper.

5.1 A back-road junction marks the entrance to the first Cotton-wood Canyon. The gravel road bends left and downhill, and two four-wheel-drive spurs go right. The right-most track goes south to Top of the World (Ride 5). Instead, take the four-wheel-drive track going east, which is part of the Dolores Overlook Trail (Ride 6).

9.8 A spur goes left; keep right. This is the 4.7-mile mark of Ride 6. Keep on this main road, ignoring all spurs. It climbs a bit farther, then heads down the second Cottonwood Canyon in a turbulent descent.

17.8 Intersect with the Onion Creek route (Ride 7) here. Onion Creek and Utah 128 are down the road to the right. Left goes to Section 5.

Across the Mesas—Section 5

0.0 Turn left, and retrace the Onion Creek route (Ride 7) to FR 033.

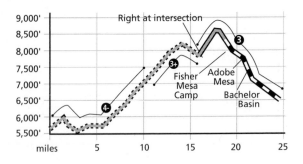

11.9 Turn right, and climb onto North Beaver Mesa.

16.2 Keep right through this intersection, which is the trailhead for Onion Creek and Polar Mesa. Gateway, Colorado, is down the road going left.

18.8 The road becomes paved. Check the brakes, and get ready for major-league speed.

18.9 The Fisher Mesa (Ride 9) trailhead is on the right.

20.9 The Adobe Mesa (Ride 10) trailhead zips by on the right.

24.2 This section is officially over where the Loop Road and Castleton Road meet.

The Home Stretch—Section 6

0.0 From the intersection of the Loop Road and Castleton Road, keep left on the Loop Road and follow the Bachelor's Bash (Ride 11) description from mile 11.3 to its trailhead.

4.6 Continue past Bachelor's Bash trailhead to climb more of the Loop Road.

5.9 Cold Springs Camp is off to the left. A few hundred yards farther and it's all downhill!

6.1 Turn right and start the descent. Look for the trail marker on the right. It's just past a pullout with a spectacular view into Castle Valley.

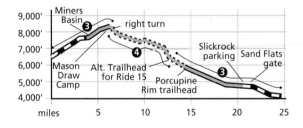

6.8 Keep right on the main trail.

7.8 Keep left to pass an old mine, avoiding the road that drops away to the right. Then keep right on the main road.

9.3 *Watch for deep ruts,* then turn right on Sand Flats Road. Stay on this road into Moab.

14.5 Porcupine Rim trailhead (Ride 15).

20.8 The Slickrock Trail (Ride 1).

24.4 Moab.

Appendix A

Additional Rides

What? You want more?!

The region offers many more rides, some of which are best discovered by finding a local, earning his or her trust, and then getting invited along. But here are some rides for when such invites are hard to come by.

In the La Sals there are a couple of nice, steep rides that leave from the Pack Creek area. It's possible to make huge loops out of these four-wheel-drive roads or to link them into high-altitude singletrack. Access them by turning right about 2 miles past Ken's Lake on the Loop Road.

Heck, grab some maps and explore La Sal Pass Road and its evil twin to the north. These are accessible via the Sheepherder's Loop (Ride 14). Also worth checking out are Lackey, Brumley, Dark Canyon Lake, Carpenter's Basin, and Black Ridge Roads. Black Ridge is directly across from the trailhead of Rides 17 and 18. That should get you started.

The Canyon Rims Recreational Area, Canyonlands Needles District, and the Abajos Mountains near Monticello also have many more rides that didn't make this book. Lockhart Basin runs from Chicken Corners (Ride 28) to Utah Highway 211 in the Needles and makes an awesome multiday trip with numerous side rides and hikes. This vast region to the south also includes the Seven Sisters Buttes, Aspen Flat, Shay Ridge, Elk Ridge, and Beef Basin rides. The Trout Water Canyon ride in the Canyon Rims Recreation Area hooks into the Boxcar Bridge route (Ride 21) for a nice loop. That'll keep you busy!

Appendix B

Resources

Moab Visitor Center
Center and Main Street
Moab, UT 84532
(800) 635–MOAB or (435)
259–8825

This is *the* place to
get almost any question
answered. They may even
know the meaning of life!
The staff includes friendly
folks from the National Park
Service, Bureau of Land
Management, and USDA
Forest Service. Try here first.

**Community Sand Flats
Team**
125 East Center Street
Moab, UT 84532
(435) 259–2444
www.grandcountyutah.net

These folks are helping to
restore and manage the area
around the Slickrock Trail.

**Bureau of Land
Management**
Moab District Office
82 East Dogwood
P.O. Box 970
Moab, UT 84523
(435) 259–2100

**Grand County Travel
Council**
P.O. Box 550
Moab, UT 84532
(800) 635–6622 or (435)
259–8825

**Canyonlands Natural
History Association**
3031 South U. S. Highway
191
Moab, UT 84532
(435) 259–6003

**Manti–La Sal National
Forest**
62 East 100 North
Moab, UT 84532
(435) 259–7155

**National Park Service—
Canyonlands Information**
Backcountry reservations:
(435) 259–4351
Information:
(435) 719–2313

**Canyonlands National
Park**
Needles District Ranger
Station
(435) 259–4711

Arches National Park
P.O. Box 907
Moab, UT 84532
(435) 719–2299

**Dead Horse Point State
Park**
Camping reservations:
(800) 322–3770
(435) 259–2614

**Utah road conditions and
weather forecast**
(801) 964–6000

Reservation Services
Moab/Canyonlands Central
Reservations:
(800) 748–4386
Infowest: (800) 576–2661
Camping information:
(800) 635–6622

Moab also exists on the
Internet. Two good starting
points are:
www.moab.net
www.moab-utah.com\start.
htm

Appendix C

Showers

Up the Creek Campground, 210 East 330 South, $4.00.

Lazy Lizard Hostel, 1213 South U.S. Highway 191, $2.00.

Moab Swim Center, 181 West 400 North, $3.00 (seasonal).

Poison Spider Bike Shop, 497 North Main, $3.00 for five minutes ($1.50 per 2½ minutes).

Slickrock Campground, 1301½ North U.S. Highway 191, $4.00.

Rustic Inn, 120 East 100 South, $3.00.

Packcreek Mobile Estates & Camp Park, 1520 Murphy Lane, $4.00.

Moab Rim Camppark, 1900 South U.S. Highway 191, $4.00.

Moab KOA, 3255 South U.S. Highway 191, $5.00.

Edge of the Desert, 1251 South Millcreek Drive, $3.00.

Canyonlands Camp Park, 555 South Main, $4.00.

Arch View Campground & Resort, U.S. Highway 191 at Utah Highway 313, $4.00.

Appendix D

Weather Info

Month	Sunrise	Sunset	High	Low	Precip
Jan	7:35	5:35	39.2	17.6	0.59
Feb	7:15	6:10	51.1	17.7	0.31
Mar	6:40	6:35	61.5	34.6	0.99
Apr	6:00	7:00	71.1	40.7	0.94
May	5:20	7:25	81.1	49.4	0.79
Jun	5:10	7:45	93.2	57.6	0.29
Jul	5:20	7:45	98.9	64.0	0.95
Aug	5:45	7:20	96.1	62.1	0.71
Sep	6:10	6:35	87.3	53.2	0.70
Oct	6:35	5:55	74.0	40.7	1.36
Nov	7:05	5:20	57.1	30.1	0.81
Dec	7:30	5:15	45.1	21.4	0.65

These are averages from 20 years worth of data. Remember, an average is a number that corresponds to nothing in reality, but it does represent a point between the extremes. Temperatures can fluctuate dramatically in the desert!

Appendix E

Camping

Once upon a time camping was free in a number of areas around Moab. The Colorado River corridor, Kane Springs, Ken's Lake, Behind the Rocks, and Sand Flats suffered from hoards that had no respect for the outdoors. Now these areas are regulated. This means it costs to camp around Moab. If you're not paying someone, chances are you're in the wrong place.

The Bureau of Land Management (BLM) now charges $5.00 for rustic site camping along the Colorado River (Utah Highway 128). The self-pay sites are marked with a tent icon on brown posts and open all year. These sites are among a number of closed sites marked with the same icon with a red circle and a slash over it. Don't even think of camping in a closed spot.

BLM Campgrounds on Utah 128 (the River Road):
Goose Island—18 sites 1.4 miles from U.S. Highway 191
Negro Bill—17 sites 3 miles from US 191
Drinks Canyon—17 sites 6.2 miles from US 191
Hal Canyon—11 sites 6.6 miles from US 191
Oak Grove—7 sites 6.9 miles from US 191
Big Bend—23 sites 8.1 miles from US 191
Upper Big Bend—8 sites 8.1 miles from US 191
Hittle Bottom—12 sites 22 miles from US 191
Dewey Bridge—7 sites 29 miles from US 191

While camping along Utah 128, you'll see strange lights illuminating the canyon walls and voices echoing down the canyon. This is only the nightly tour that floats down the river complete with PA system and spotlight-equipped support vehicles.

If your camp area doesn't have a trash bin, pack out your trash to neighboring Goose Island and Big Bend Campsites.

BLM Campgrounds on Utah Highway 279 (near Rides 31 and 32):

Jay Cee Park—7 sites 4 miles west of US 191
GoldBar—10 sites 10 miles west of US 191

BLM Campgrounds on Kane Creek Road:

Kings Bottom—7 sites 2.8 miles west of US 191
MoonFlower—8 sites 3 miles west of US 191
Hunters Canyon—9 sites 7.8 miles west of US 191 (on dirt road)
Echo—9 sites 8 miles west of US 191 (on dirt road)

Other Area BLM Campgrounds:

Sand Flats Recreation Area—143 sites 2 miles east of Moab (see Appendix F)
Ken's Lake—31 sites 8.5 miles from US 191 (see access directions for Ride 16)
Windwhistle—15 sites 32 miles south of Moab on US 191, then west 6 miles on Needles Overlook Road.

Other Nonprivate Campgrounds:

La Sal National Forest

Warner Lake Campground—20 seasonal sites on La Sal Loop Road (in mountains) 24 miles from Moab

Arches National Park

Devils Garden—53 sites

Canyonlands National Park

Needles District—26 sites (near Rides 22 and 23)

Island in the Sky District—12 sites (near Rides 32, 33, and 41)

Dead Horse Point State Park

21 RV sites 31 miles from Moab on Utah Highway 313 (near Rides 32, 33, and 41)

Private Campgrounds:

Archview campground—US 191 at Utah 313; (800) 813-6622, (435) 259-7854 (seasonal)

Canyonlands Campground—555 South Main Street; (800) 522-6848, (435) 259-6848

Dowd Flats RV Park—2701 South US 191; (435) 259-5909

Edge of the Desert—1251 South Millcreek Drive; (435) 259-3337

Kane Springs Campground—1705 Kane Creek Road; (435) 259-7821 (seasonal)

Lions Back Camp Park—Sandflats Road west of Sandflats Recreation Area; (435) 259-7954

Moab KOA—3225 South US 191; (800) 562-0372, (435) 259-6682 (seasonal)

Moab Rim Campark—1900 South US 191; (888) 599-6622, (435) 259-5002 (seasonal)

Moab Valley RV & Campark—1773 South US 191; (435) 259-4469 (seasonal)

OK RV Park & Canyonlands Stables—3310 Spanish Valley Road; (435) 259-1400

Pack Creek Campground—1520 Murphy Lane, #6; (435) 259-2982

Portal RV Park & Fishery—1261 North US 191; (800) 574-2028, (435) 259-6108

Riverside Oasis—1861 North US 191; (877) 285-7757, (435) 259-3424 (seasonal)

Slickrock Campground—1301½ North US 191; (800) 448-8873, (435) 259-2411

Spanish Trail RV Park—2980 South US 191; (800) 787-2751, (435) 259-2411 (seasonal)

Up the Creek—210 East 300 South in Moab; (435) 259-6995 (seasonal)

Appendix F

Sand Flats Recreational Area

To access Slickrock Trail (Ride 1) and Porcupine Rim (Ride 15) or camp along Sand Flats Road, you must pay a fee. If there isn't anyone in the entrance house, use the self-pay station.

Before you grumble too much about this, you should know how bad the area was becoming before fees were charged. The anarchy that was Sand Flats wasn't good for the land. Now the area is managed by the Community Sand Flats Team, and things are looking good. Besides, the fees are extremely low.

It costs $5.00 for a car to enter. If you ride in by bike, it costs $2.00. If you take a shuttle in, you still owe your $2.00 at the gate though the shuttle driver may have already charged you (find out). The pass (your receipt) is good for three days. If that's not good enough, you can buy an annual pass for a mere $20.

At the entrance gate is a message board and information kiosk. This is a great place to meet up with fellow bikers. By the way, another such message board is at Eddie McStiff's next to the Moab Visitor Center.

There are 143 campsites up here. Each site costs $8.00 per vehicle, which covers four people. It costs $2.00 more per additional person, and the sites have a limit of ten people. Campers have a checkout time of 1:00 P.M. As a courtesy to other campers, a 10:00 P.M. to 6:00 A.M. quiet time is in effect. The sites are in clusters that have toilets but no trash bins. Trash should be packed out or placed in the bins located at the Slickrock Trail trailed.

There is absolutely no gathering or cutting of firewood or tinder. That gnarled juniper log is part of the desert environment. Fires are allowed in the metal fire rings with wood you brought with you. Firewood is available in town at City Market or most gas stations/convienence stores.

Glossary

ATB: All-terrain bicycle; aka mountain bike, sprocket rocket, fat-tire flyer.

ATV: All-terrain vehicle; in this book ATV refers to motorbikes and three- and four-wheelers designed for off-road use.

Bail: Getting off the bike, usually in a hurry and whether or not you meant to. Often a last resort.

Bunny hop: Leaping up, while riding, and lifting both wheels off the ground to jump over an obstacle (or for sheer joy).

Clean: To ride without touching a foot (or other body part) to the ground; to ride a tough section successfully.

Clipless: A type of pedal with a binding that accepts a special cleat on the soles of bike shoes. The cleat clicks in for more control and efficient pedaling, and out for safe landings (in theory).

Contour: A line on a topographic map showing a continuous elevation level over uneven ground. Also used as a verb to indicate a fairly easy or moderate grade: "The trail contours around the canyon rim before the final grunt to the top."

Dab: To put a foot or hand down (or hold onto or lean on a tree or other support) while riding. If you have to dab, then you haven't ridden that piece of trail **clean.**

Downfall: Trees that have fallen across the trail.

Doubletrack: A trail, jeep road, ATV route, or other track with two distinct ribbons of **tread,** typically with grass growing in between. No matter which side you choose, the other rut always looks smoother.

Endo: Lifting the rear wheel off the ground and riding (or abruptly not riding) on the front wheel only. Also known, at various degrees of control and finality, as a nose wheelie, "going over the handlebars," and a face plant.

Fall line: The angle and direction of a slope; the **line** you follow when gravity is in control and you aren't.

Graded: When a gravel road is scraped level to smooth out the washboards and potholes, it has been *graded*. In this book a road is listed as graded only if it is regularly maintained. Not all such roads are graded every year, however.

Granny gear: The lowest (easiest) gear, a combination of the smallest of the three chainrings on the bottom bracket spindle (where the pedals and crank arms attach to the bike's frame) and the largest cog on the rear cluster. Shift down to your granny gear for serious climbing.

Hammer: To ride hard; derived from how it feels afterward: "I'm hammered."

Hammerhead: Someone who actually enjoys feeling **hammered.** A Type A personality rider who goes hard and fast all the time.

Line: The route (or trajectory) between or over obstacles or through turns. **Tread** or trail refers to the ground you're riding on; the line is the path you choose within the tread (and exists mostly in the eye of the beholder).

Off-the-seat: Moving your butt behind the bike seat and over the rear tire; used for control on extremely steep descents. This position increases braking power, helps prevent **endos,** and reduces skidding.

Portage: To carry the bike, usually up a steep hill, across unrideable obstacles, or through a stream.

Quads: Thigh muscles (short for quadraceps); or maps in the USGS topographic series (short for quadrangles). Nice quads of either kind can help get you out of trouble in the back-country.

Ratcheting: Also known as backpedaling; pedaling backward to avoid hitting rocks or other obstacles with pedals.

Sidehill: Where the trail crosses a slope. If the **tread** is narrow, keep your inside (uphill) pedal up to avoid hitting the ground. If the tread tilts downhill, you may have to use some body language to keep the bike plumb or vertical to avoid slipping out.

Singletrack: A trail, game run, or other track with only one ribbon of **tread.** But this is like defining an orgasm as a muscle cramp. Good singletrack is pure fun.

Spur: A side road or trail that splits off from the main route.

Surf: Riding through loose gravel or sand, when the wheels sway from side to side. Also *heavy surf:* frequent and difficult obstacles.

Suspension: A bike with front suspension has a shock-absorbing fork or stem. Rear suspension absorbs shock between the rear wheel and frame. A bike with both is said to be fully suspended.

Switchbacks: When a trail goes up a steep slope, it zigzags or *switchbacks* across the **fall line** to ease the gradient of the climb. Well-designed switchbacks make a turn with at least an 8-foot radius and remain fairly level within the turn itself. These are rare, however, and cyclists often struggle to ride through sharply angled, sloping switchbacks.

Track stand: Balancing on a bike in one place, without rolling forward appreciably. Cock the front wheel to one side and bring that pedal up to the one or two o'clock position. Now control your side-to-side balance by applying pressure on the pedals and brakes and changing the angle of the front wheel, as needed. It takes practice but really comes in handy at stoplights, on **switchbacks,** and when trying to free a foot before falling.

Tread: The riding surface, particularly regarding **single-track.**

Water bar: A log, rock, or other barrier placed in the **tread** to divert water off the trail and prevent erosion. Peeled logs can be slippery and cause bad falls, especially when they angle sharply across the trail.

A Short Index of Rides

17. Prostitute Behind the Rocks
20. Flat Iron Mesa
22. Colorado River Overlook
26. Hurrah Pass
30. Beneath the Wires
33. Gemini Bridges (with shuttle)
41. White Rim

Technical Tests
1. The Slickrock Trail
5. Top of the World
12. Burro Pass
13. Moonlight Meadow
14. Sheepherder's Loop—Trans La Sal option
15. Porcupine Rim
16. Flat Pass
18. Behind the Rocks Trail
24. Pritchett Arch to Gatherer's Canyon
25. Amasa Back
29. Moab Rim
31. Poison Spider Mesa and the Portal Trail
36. Tusher Canyon's Left Side
37. Tusher Too—Tusher Canyon's Right Side
38. Bartlett Wash
40. Gold Bar Rim

Great Climbs—the Yearn to Burn
1. The Slickrock Trail
4. Pole Canyon Rim
5. Top of the World
6. Dolores River Overlook

9. Fisher Mesa
10. Adobe Mesa
11. Bachelor's Bash
12. Burro Pass
14. Sheepherder's Loop
25. Amasa Back
27. Jackson Hole
28. Chicken Corners
29. Moab Rim
32. Jug Handle Loop—The Shafer Trail
40. Gold Bar Rim
41. White Rim
42. The Kokopelli Trail

Great Downhills—the Need for Speed
4. Pole Canyon Rim
5. Top of the World
6. Dolores River Overlook
7. Onion Creek
9. Fisher Mesa
10. Adobe Mesa
11. Bachelor's Bash
12. Burro Pass
14. Sheepherder's Loop
15. Porcupine Rim
27. Jackson Hole
28. Chicken Corners
32. Jug Handle Loop—The Shafer Trail
33. Gemini Bridges

Epic Rides—a Day in the Saddle

About the Author

David Crowell is a professional writer and photographer with a passion for the outdoors and a penchant for mountain biking and surfing. He has written numerous books, including *Mountain Biking Colorado Springs, Exploring Southern California's Beaches,* and *Exploring Capital Reef National Park,* each of which are FalconGuides. He left Colorado to surf and now lives in Ventura, California, with his wife, Heidi, and their son, Dawson.